Laptop Entrepreneur

Realistic Ways You Can Live the Dream Abroad and Make Money Online

Ryan Scott Shannon

Copyright © 2020 Ryan Scott Shannon

All rights reserved.

ISBN: 9798619205985

CONTENTS

1	You, Too, Can Become Location-Independent	Pg 1
2	How Being a Laptop Entrepreneur Pays Off	Pg 11
3	Traits That Make a Successful Laptop Entrepreneur	Pg 21
4	Common Laptop Entrepreneur Business Models	Pg 25
5	Remote Work Contracts	Pg 28
6	Using a Freelancing Platform	Pg 33
7	Working Independently as a Freelancer	Pg 44
8	Operating a Virtual	Pg

	Business	52
	Dropshipping	
	Blogging	
	Influencer Marketing	
	Selling a Physical Product Online	
	Selling e-Products	
	Property Rentals	
9	Don't Limit Yourself - Set Your Own Schedule and Be Free	Pg 109

1 You, Too, Can Become Location- Independent and Own Your Schedule

If you're like most people, chances are you're stressed, tired and overworked right now (be honest with yourself: aren't you?). In fact, research from Everest College found that, "83% of US workers suffer from work-related stress" (Stress.org, Milenkovic, 2019). And, even more worrying, "94% of American workers report experiencing stress at their workplace" (Stress.org, Milenkovic, 2019). If you weren't stressed about your job, you probably wouldn't have been intrigued by this book. You wouldn't be researching ways to make money online. That's because with the current employment system, you're expected to clock in at 9 am and leave at 5 pm. But what does that really mean? It means sacrificing eight hours of your day - approximately 50% of your waking hours - spent at work. Eight hours each and every day, forty hours a week that you'll never get back. And, that excludes the time it takes you to commute, shower, and get ready. But, does it need to be like this? Are we really made to spend most of our time tucked away in offices and preparing ourselves for the next work day? I don't think so. I have found a way to make money online that allows me two things far more valuable than money: **freedom** and **flexibility**.

If you're working a regular full-time job, let's be honest: you're chained to your schedule. Your morning commute (that you hate); your waking hour, the time you fall asleep; what you make for breakfast, lunch and dinner; how much time you spend with friends and family is all dictated by your work schedule. You really don't want to drive across town, but of course, you have to because you need to keep your job. You can't eat as healthy as you'd like, but the sugar-laced protein bar and tall coffee (with lots of sugar added, of course) is convenient and prevents you from dozing off in front of your computer. You're naturally a night owl, but that doesn't work when your alarm clock is set at 8 am. You probably aren't getting a full night's sleep anyway.

Let's go through what a typical work-centered schedule looks like:

Wake up early in the morning. You may lay in bed from exhaustion, hitting snooze several times. You just don't have the energy - or the will - to get out of bed. Or, maybe you decide to mindlessly scroll social media to take your mind off things (you think to yourself subconsciously: it's going to be another long day!).

Get ready in a rush. Maybe throw on some makeup or some gel in your hair. Or, maybe you don't - your boss isn't paying you to look good, right? You may pack a lunch. Or not. You know it's not good for you, but you'll opt for a snack from the vending machine or order some fast food out of convenience. There just aren't enough hours in the day, right?

Head to work before rush hour. Or maybe you get caught in rush hour... this isn't going to look good. Your boss is going to wonder why you're late. You finally get there (hopefully on time) only after stressing about being on time, spiking your cortisol levels (which leads to chronic inflammation overtime - that means early aging, a weakened immune system and a higher chance of chronic illness).

Work, work, work. If you're lucky, the time passes quickly. You get involved with what you're doing, but you realize you're still making money for someone else. You have a lot of potential - and you know it - but you just don't have the time or the resources to go virtual as a Laptop Entrepreneur (or so you think!).

Back home, exhausted and stressed. You finally get back home and hit the couch...but wait - you haven't eaten dinner yet. And the kids! What about the kids?! You need to make sure everything and everyone is taken care of first. And of course, you need to tell a friend or loved one about how your boss is driving you crazy and how your co-workers aren't being all that helpful, too. You're stressed and have to take care of others before you take care of yourself.

And finally: you watch the news and doze off. Not only are you stressed from work itself, stressed about getting to work on time, and stressed about making dinner for yourself and others, you then need to stress about the news, too. There's always something new to stress about: Oh no, another war. Or, oh jeez another viral outbreak. While it's important to keep current events on your radar, it may not be in your best interest to listen to several different commentators beat the same dead horse over and over again. And maybe you get that - you opt for Netflix instead. The only problem is, somewhere deep inside of you, you know you were created for more. You have hobbies, interests, and passions. But you're far too busy and exhausted to pursue those. Instead of learning how to paint, or finishing that book you've always wanted to write, or going out for a hike to watch the sunset, you'd rather tune out and watch your favorite TV series. Your life now is centered around work. Even on weekends, you sleep in to recover. You may binge drink to forget about the stress. And that's not living life to your **true potential.**

How Your Day Can Look As a Laptop Entrepreneur

Isn't the common routine stressful? Raise your hand if that looks like your routine. I know that that's a common routine for many of you. Other factors that contribute to stress are: bosses, high work-loads and poor communication (Stress.org, Milenkovic, 2019). I know that that's a common routine for many of you. In fact, that was how my routine looked, too! Fortunately, when I was in university in Italy, I learned I had another option: I could make money online. But, I learned this the hard way. I was trying to make ends meet while studying full-time (fortunately, I've outlined everything for you and taught you valuable lessons I've learned from my mistakes. That way, you can choose a Laptop Entrepreneur business model that works for you).

Being a Laptop Entrepreneur means full autonomy over your schedule and life. That means you can kiss your 30-minute commute goodbye along with your worries about being late to work! Now, when you commit to living like a Laptop Entrepreneur, you finally have flexibility and a little bit less stress and peace of mind (which we all need!). Being a Laptop Entrepreneur means fitting your schedule to your life, whereas being a worker means finding a way to fit your life in between the gaps in your work schedule. That's the difference.

So how does a typical day for a Laptop Entrepreneur look?

Wake up on your schedule. Had a long night? That's totally OK. Instead of worrying about work the next day and clocking in on time, you realize you can finally sleep in and recover your sleep debt you've accumulated. Since starting your own virtual business, you realize you set the rules for your own schedule. Or, if you decided to negotiate with your boss and make your current position one that is digital, you agree that you can work whenever you want - as long as you're pulling your weight.

Work more productively in a tranquil environment. It may be counterintuitive, but workers are more productive at home than they are in the office. When people set up a designated distraction-free area in their home to work, they're more likely to get into a "workflow" state. That means getting more done and finally catching up on lagging projects - without Suzy from the cubicle next to taking you out of your focused state.

You get work done - and then you clock out. An amazing thing that Laptop Entrepreneurs often find is that they're able to accomplish their daily goals during their working hours so they no longer have to think about work outside of work. And that's so stress relieving. That means work time is work time and playtime is playtime - no more negative work thoughts robbing you of your precious freetime.

You involve yourself with a few hobbies. Now that you've snipped off your commute and are working four days a week instead of five, you now decide to walk in the park more often, or play with your kids, or you decide to join your local softball team. You also don't need to talk and complain much about work anymore since you're hitting your goals in your distraction-free workplace. Plus, you're making more meals at home with whole foods and now have more energy.

Your weekends are fulfilling and relaxing. Instead of spending your mornings (and, let's be honest: most of your afternoon!) on the couch or in bed watching TV, you no longer need to sleep in and have those lazy days to recover from the work week. And, if you still love your lazy days as a Laptop Entrepreneur, you don't feel guilty about taking them. You decide when you need to rest and you don't need to cram errands you couldn't get to during the work week on Saturday and Sunday.

You now understand what work-life balance is. You may have read an article on what work-life balance is and think you have a general concept of what it is, but you'll never fully reap the benefits until you become a Laptop Entrepreneur. You already try to turn your email off when you're off duty at work, you try to turn the TV off early and try to spend time with your family, but sometimes checking your email is too necessary - and addictive - and you're too exhausted to visit your parents or play with your kids. Ultimately, you can try to implement some "work-life balance" tips and tricks, but you'll never really **own** your schedule until you go virtual.

You generate money. Since most of the methods of being a Laptop Entrepreneur involve working for yourself (with the exception of negotiating virtual working hours with your employer), you're no longer interested in trading your time for money. Instead, you trade the value you produce for money. Or, you trade products for money. You trade your knowledge for money. That's what we call "generating" an income instead of being paid a set salary of wage. Even if you're working hard and pulling more than your weight at work, your efforts may go unnoticed. That means no bonus, no salary increase.

Working online as a freelancer, on the other hand, often means specializing in a certain area and delivering a virtual good or service. You don't get paid by the hour; rather by what you've produced. Let's say you agree to write product descriptions for sellers on Amazon; if you charge $100 for a fully optimized listing, and it takes you one hour to write and research, you've now earned $100 per hour (obviously). If it takes you two hours, you've made $50 per hour. The point is: you're being paid based on the value you deliver, not on how long it takes you (which can mean making more money than a traditional workplace setting). And, if you want to make passive income by selling products online (both digital and physical products), there are strategies for that, too, which I've outlined further in the book.

I don't think it takes much elaboration: any sane person would prefer a life that's less stressful, allowing for more free time than a life that's just work, work, work. We weren't designed to be hidden inside all day - there's so much more to life than just making a living. The great thing about being a Laptop Entrepreneur is that it can be done from anywhere! That means you can choose to work from the comfort of your own home, or you may decide to join some of the tens of thousands who have become Digital Nomads. As a Laptop Entrepreneur, you can finally see the world like you've always wanted to. You've always been the type to sift through National Geographic magazines, hoping some day to visit those far-off places. But, you've got a job, obligations and don't have enough vacation days. Guess what? When you become a Laptop Entrepreneur, every day is a vacation (or, more accurately: a workation. You will have to put in some work, which I'll go over later, but it simply means putting in the work when **you** want to)!

Why Being a Laptop Entrepreneur Pairs Well With Travel

Here we are in the 21st century. When we think of nomads, we may think of ancient tribes scavenging the Earth trying to survive day to day, tied to no fixed place. Nomads often migrate based on the season, opting to head south in the winter, where the climate's a bit warmer, and north in the summer, where they can return to their home base. Or, they may follow their flock of sheep or goats, letting the livestock decide where they're led to next in pursuit of more vegetation and fresher pastures.

In essence, not much has changed. Instead of walking stalves and grass shacks, we now wield laptops and book Airbnbs. But, much like our ancestors, we follow the sun. Imagine living in Norway during the winter, getting only a few hours of daylight and being greeted by bone-chilling winds upon leaving your house. Many of us migrate down south in the wintertime as "snow birds" to ride out the cold, sullen winter. We chase after grass that's much greener online instead of hoping to grow in a company that may never give you the salary you could potentially earn being your own boss.

People are increasingly electing to choose a homeless lifestyle that's not anchored to any particular place. Constantly drifting wherever life decides to take you next. In reality, homeless is exactly what Digital Nomads and many Laptop Entrepreneurs are. Or, rather, house-less. Many realize home isn't a physical destination, but rather, is a feeling often tied to the people you reside with. Being homeless isn't necessarily a bad thing. It doesn't always mean you're a drug-addicted panhandler laying on the side of the street anymore. Rather, it's a person who's broken free from a traditional lifestyle and has decided not to cement themselves into a single place. What this means can vary among digital nomads. Some digital nomads choose to set up bases around the world where they return to often. For example, you may set up a base in your hometown to see your friends' and family's smiling faces a few times per year, but then opt to ride out the colder winter months in a more temperate climate, say Bali or Phuket.

For others, being "homeless" as a Digital Nomad means being constantly on the go. These are the types of people who want to see as much of the world as they can. Preferably as fast as possible, fueled *fernweh* (meaning an intense desire to travel in German). There are other Laptop Entrepreneurs who opt for a more slowed-down, leisurely pace of travel. Rather than rushing around the world from one plane, train or car, these types of nomads wade through the face of the Earth, marinating in the local culture, stopping to smell the roses more often along the road. Not to mention, this option often burns through the wallet the slowest. It's cheaper to rent a room for an entire month than book different Airbnbs every few nights.

And again: being a Laptop Entrepreneur doesn't necessarily mean living on the go. You're not required to travel if you make money online. While I've focused the next section on capitalizing on the advantage of living in countries with lower costs of living, it's also important to keep in mind that working remotely also allows you to stay planted where you are. That is to say: if there's ever been a point in your life where you've moved for a job, you don't need to do that. You can live where you want as a Laptop Entrepreneur. Do you really desire living in a quiet suburb? Or, perhaps somewhere rural, in a tiny home for example? As long as you have good wifi, and implement one of the Laptop Entrepreneur business strategies, these options are entirely possible for you. Many are choosing to live the laptop entrepreneur lifestyle because it grants them more time to spend with their family. In fact, as you'll discover further in the Blogging section further in the book, 'Mommy' blogs are one of the most popular - and lucrative - blogging topics, usually run by (you guessed it!) moms. Creating a second income as a stay-at-home mom is why so many moms are choosing to become laptop entrepreneurs. Some of them become so successful, they grow their part-time income into a fully-fledged income that's enough to provide for their entire family - alon! Others, like me, have decided to stop trading time for dollars. If you're like me, you hate clocking in at a traditional 40-hours-a-week. It's not that I don't like to work or that I'm an entitled millennial; rather, I'd rather work for myself and prioritize my health, passions, and flexibility in my schedule over making a stable paycheck each week. We're only on this earth for about 80 years or so (hopefully more now that we're living less stressful lives as laptop entrepreneurs!). So why would I want to be cooped up in an office five days out of seven?

We give up the most prime hours, seasons, days and years of our lives in exchange for a paycheck. We don't even see the sun most days - we're too busy pecking away at our computers inside! There's got to be a different way to this modern slavery system. I've wondered about an alternative and so have you (that's why you picked this book). And, a solution exists! The answer for people looking to make decent money (and potentially millions each year!) is to ditch the traditional expectation of wasting most of your waking hours making someone else's money, and instead paving your own digital path online!

2 How Being A Laptop Entrepreneur Pays Off

Why do people choose to pick up and live life on the go? Are they crazy or unhappy with their current location? What's driving this ever-increasing trend? While the desire to travel the world and make an income on the go can be personal and vary from each individual, there are a few factors that drive people to pack their bags with a carry-on and their dreams! Here are seven reasons it makes sense to become a Digital Nomad:

1. Saving Money (Pull Factor). Imagine having the ability to increase your purchasing power 5-fold or more! That's exactly what some Digital Nomads aim for when they embark on their adventure around the world. A lower cost of living means saving a higher portion of your income. Saving money is a huge factor that lures people into the Digital Nomad tribe (as it has for me!). By traveling to places that have a lower cost of living than your current location, you can afford to increase your standard of living. A beachfront bungalow, fancy cocktails in coconut shells and eating fresh seafood is a lot cheaper in Phuket than Miami, for example. And that's the whole idea. Getting the same (or sometimes better) quality for a lot less. The lower cost of living allows Digital Nomads to save up or vastly improve their standard of living. It's simple economics; getting paid in a higher-valued currency (the Euro, US Dollar, British pound, etc.) and living in a country that has a lower-valued currency equals huge savings. Looking at the Cost of Living Index below from Numbeo.com, we see that Switzerland ranks relatively high. On the opposite spectrum, Georgia (the country, not the state) ranks quite low. By transferring from Bern to Batumi, you'd reduce your costs by 83.08%. To put that in perspective, the average net monthly salary in Bern is $5,347.79 with the average expenditure (including rent) for one person is USD $2,436.77. This means approximately 45.56% of your net income goes to expenses. Meanwhile, transferring to Batumi (with the same average salary) where the cost of living plus rent only costs roughly USD $600, you'd be able to save $4,747.79, which is significantly higher than your savings in Bern.

2. Rising Cost of Living in Western Countries (Push Factor). For many in the West, it's not all glitz and glam. While we're stereotyped for being rich by others (especially in the third world), the reality is, we face more expenses and taxes (that seem to be ever-growing!). Many Westerners are finding it increasingly difficult to keep up with rent and expenses. The U.S. poverty rate stands at 12.3%; a significant portion of the population. And that doesn't include the middle class; many are bogged down by *mortgages, debt, student loans and healthcare expenses* for chronic illnesses like cancer (U.S. Census Bureau, 2017). High living expenses isn't exclusive to the U.S., either. Exploring other countries in the Anglosphere, the average net salary in the UK is $2,302, however, the average expenses for a single person in London (renting a central 1 bedroom apartment) come out to be USD $3,2111.28 (Numbeo.com, 2020). This means living in London would require you to take out USD $1,000 each month in savings if you're paid an average UK salary and living in London. This could force you into finding roommates and cutting back on food and other expenses, leaving virtually no room for savings. Looking at Sydney, Australia, there's a similar "crowding out" effect where the cost of living plus rent leaves no room for savings and causes residents to sacrifice their lifestyle (i.e. eating lower quality foods, shopping for cheap hygienic products, etc.) to keep up with expenses. The average monthly net salary in Sydney is USD $3,404.85, meanwhile, rent and expenses for a single person add up to be USD $2,704.94. While this leaves an average of around USD $700 each month, many would prefer to live in a country where they could stretch their monthly savings to eventually afford a house in Sydney; home to the second most unaffordable housing in the world, costing 12.2 times the median income (Demographia, 2019).

3. **Escaping the Rat Race.** For many of us in the West, life has already been mapped out for us. We're led to believe we must follow the status quo and work a 9-to-5 job. The indoctrination starts young: you need to get good grades to get into a good university. After university, you need to get a good job. And of course, after working at your good job for several decades, you need to save to live a good retirement. In an extreme example, the German education system already begins to differentiate the factions of society by age 10: *Gymnasium* for top-performing students on track to attend university, *Realschule* for average students who should go on to achieve white-collar careers, and *Hauptschule* for the lowest-ranking students who will likely become laborers or blue-collar workers. Crunching the numbers on the 'Rat Race' lifestyle, you spend 8 hours sleeping, 8 hours working, 2 hours cooking and eating, and let's say 1 hour commuting. That only leaves you 5 hours to really *live* (and of course, after working 8 hours, so many are too tired to pursue their passions so they plop themselves on the couch and tune out with Netflix). But does it need to be this way? Your life may have already been mapped out for you, but fortunately,

the Laptop Entrepreneur lifestyle allows people to redraw the lines of their own destinies.

Laptop Entrepreneurs and Digital Nomads are individuals that are creative and innovative enough to realize fitting the cookie-cutter mold in life doesn't guarantee happiness and success. Education systems and jobs tend to put people in boxes, making people think their life and value are centered around how much they make, what they studied or where they went to school. Escaping the rat race means pursuing your passions, not your desired income. It means valuing free time over making more money with overtime. It means riding the waves of life as you work, rather than working up to save for that vacation you've been needing all year. Ultimately, Digital Nomads, "often define themselves based more on their specific leisure interests and orientation—beach and surfing, mountain climbing, or snowboarding—rather than focus on an identity based on their specific type of remote work that supports their lifestyle" (Blackshaw 2018, 80).

4. Wanderlust. Some people naturally have a desire to explore and become acquainted with the world. Digital Nomads tend to be these types of people. Wanting to see the world has swept the entire Millennial generation. In fact, "74 percent of Americans now prioritize experiences over products or things" and, "65 percent of millennials are currently saving money to travel, which is more than the average for other generations" (Forbes.com, Morgan, 2019). This is a worldwide phenomenon; consumers are becoming less attached to things and brands and are instead seeking out meaningful experiences - like travel. Going out and seeing the world is one of the most transformative, educational experiences one can take. Traveling shifts you out of your comfort zone and submerges you into foreign lands, which leads you to question the culture in which you grew up and even auto-analyze yourself. While staying in your home country, everything is normal. When you transcend cultural barriers and emerge on foreign lands, your perception of normal expands. You see people living life in a completely different way that works - but is completely different than your own. After seeing the ways of others, you may even decide to adopt some of their practices (for example: the bidet in Italy! I'm never turning back), or you may grow to appreciate the culture you grew up in even more when you see the uglier side of things (i.e. dirty streets, contaminated water, etc.)

5. Flexible Schedule. Who doesn't want a little more wiggle room in their schedule? That's what being a Digital Nomad is all about. It's not just centered around location independence; freedom in one's schedule is just as important, too. Many people think being a Digital Nomad is focused around working from anywhere in the world (which does play a large part) but just as important is deciding *when* you work. There are varying types of Laptop Entrepreneur models, which I'll cover below, that have varying types of schedule flexibility. There are a variety of factors that determine how rigid your schedule is, including: whether you decide to pair up with a freelancing platform or go the independent route, whether you decide to take on more clients or opt for working with a select few, and whether you decide to outsource work or do it all yourself. Another factor to consider is differences in time zones. If your clients are located halfway around the world, you may have to get up earlier than usual or stay up a bit later to work on your laptop at night or attend a virtual meeting on Skype. But ultimately, being a Digital Nomad allows you to decide whether you want to keep the 9 to 5 working hours (from your own home, or around the world), work the night owl shift, work 60 hours a week - or 20. Your schedule is all in your hands.

Schedule customization isn't something that's exclusive to remote workers, either. There has been an increasing demand for traditional in-office workers to have more control over their schedules. In previous decades, there has been a more hard-lined, Tayloristic approach to managing a company. Now, more and more business leaders are adopting a management system that values human emotions, utilizing soft skills to lead a team of people. It's well established that more satisfied employees lead to higher productivity and company loyalty. By letting employees pick out when they work, many employers are reaping huge benefits. And, best of all, employees are satisfied, too. Take Sweden, for example. One 20-employee company was able to double its revenue after adopting a 6-hour workday. While they initially had concerns over reduced employee output and considered the possibility of having to hire new employees, they found, "a shorter workday can reduce turnover, enhance employee creativity and lift productivity enough to offset the cost of hiring additional staff." While this was for a search engine optimization (SEO) start-up, the results have also been reproduced in other areas, too. This phenomena was also experienced in the medical field as well. Despite having to hire 15 new workers, Sahlgrenska University Hospital's Orthopedics department found that their productivity and scope of services increased with shorter working hours, too: "The unit is performing 20 percent more operations, generating additional business from treatments like hip replacements that would have gone to other hospitals. Surgery waiting times were cut to weeks from months, allowing patients to return to work faster and reducing sick leave elsewhere in the economy" (Silva). This further demonstrates the demand that workers have for more flexibility and freedom in their schedule and why Laptop Entrepreneurs and traditional employees can benefit alike in a more customized, flexible schedule.

6. Incentive From Employer. While working from home or remotely may seem to benefit the employee more than the employer, there are some undeniable benefits for the employer to start allowing workers to work from home. It's been well established that happier workers means more productive workers, and working from home would lead to happiness for many. But there's more to it than that. Aside from these externalities of increased productivity due to improved employee morale, there are real tangible benefits employees can directly benefit from - and many companies are realizing this. There's already a growing trend in (mainly tech) companies called 'Work At Home Fridays'. Why would companies allow their workers to work at home - especially tech companies? Aren't they worried about employers slacking off and dropping productivity? No; it turns out they aren't. On top of the fact that work-from-home models boost productivity by ten to twenty percent, 25% of remote workers report less stress while 36% would choose to work at home *over a raise*, if given the option. But, there are also measurable cost-saving benefits for the employer, too. This includes: saving money on gas allowances. Some businesses allow employees to commute on their dime, paying for subway tickets or allowing a gasoline allowance. No commute means saving both money and time. This also benefits the environment and can work to reduce pollution and congestion on the roads. 80% of workers in the United States of America drive in a car alone; if there's no need to drive to work, this could help cut down on CO_2 emissions and $PM10$ as well as $PM2.5$ pollutants. On top of that, "78% of managers think that flexible working hours help retain and motivate important staff members." This translates into attracting more high-quality applicants and demonstrates a modern, people-first company culture.

7. **Unconventional Entrepreneurial Opportunities.** Instead of setting up a brick and mortar shop, Laptop Entrepreneurs now have the power to set up shop entirely from their laptop. That means no inventory to manage directly, no physical shop (i.e. no rent) and no customers to deal with face-to-face (perfect for introverts like me!). The virtual marketplace has allowed anyone from anywhere to access the power of the internet and generate an income entirely online. And, best

of all - there are many options that have low to no capital requirements. That's right - you don't need any startup funds to start making money online. Take working on a freelance platform, for example (which I'll cover further below). No money is required to start working on sites like Fiverr and Upwork. All you need is a bit of gray matter and some in-demand skills. Or, starting your own dropshipping site, which involves creating a user-friendly website in which customers can buy products - all while outsourcing the shipping. This is often done with products from AliExpress. Many successful drop shippers haven't even seen the products they sell - they use marketing skills to help connect the right products with the right buyers. Dropshipping only requires a website, which isn't very expensive (around $20 per year). Yet another example of a low-investment business model you can start now! When you become a Digital Nomad, you join the club of entrepreneurs who are continuing to shape the economy and influence consumer habits. We live in a technological age; there are no geographic limits anymore and low barriers to entry! By putting in a bit of work and creating value, you don't have to rely on an employer anymore. Working online means complete self-sufficiency - from anywhere in the world.

As mentioned above, working from home, or on the road, isn't easy. While it may seem a little risky and even scary to start your own journey working from home, to put things in perspective, you should be more scared of wasting your youth, or wasting precious moments with your family, or spending your health on a job that stresses you. That, to me, is more scary than potentially failing to launch a virtual business (though I discuss ways to mitigate risk and ensure your chance of success is high). The laptop entrepreneur lifestyle allows anyone with a bit of drive and entrepreneurship to put their passions, personal schedule and health on the top of their life priorities - and not some job that earns you little pieces of paper. That's not to say you won't have to work or that you won't make much money - you **will** work and you

can make lots of money. It's just that for most laptop entrepreneurs, that's not the entire goal. It's a byproduct of reaching the ultimate goal in life. And what would that be? What's the main goal for most Laptop Entrepreneurs? Freedom and flexibility. When you decide to become a Laptop Entrepreneur, you're deciding to put **you** first, not your job.

But, you'll only be free and have a flexible schedule if you put in a little sweat equity first. There are options that require a bit more "activation energy" (i.e. working hard - and more importantly: strategically - to create value before you start making money online) while other options are ready for you to start working from home right away. The point is: you'll be working on your terms; on your watch. Which option you take depends on your interests, where you're at in life and how entrepreneurial you are. For example, I have been using freelancing platforms (both Fiverr and Upwork) for a few years to help pay my way through university. While I was in school full-time, I decided it'd be too much for me to take on creating my own website, developing my own products, etc. (even though that;s my ultimate goal and the option that has the highest profit potential). So, I opted for utilizing a freelancing platform instead, which was more turn-key and allowed me to build my portfolio. However, now that I'm graduated and have more time on my hands, I'll be focusing on creating a virtual business and furthering the SEO consulting and digital marketing services I'm offering on my own website (at RyanScottSEO.com).

Looking at another stressful and busy scenario, if you're a stay-at-home mother and are caring for a newborn, you'll likely be too sleep deprived to learn and research the best virtual business to get into. Instead, you may decide to ask your employer in a traditional setting to allow you to work from home - and maybe even for less hours. That way, you can split up your schedule however you want - you can even take a few hours break in the middle of the day and go to the park, or spend time cooking a nutritious meal instead of grabbing something cheap, fast and unhealthy as many do during their lunch hour at the office. Or, you may be in your 50's working at a job you hate and now you've decided to do something radical: quit your job, live off your savings for a while and start an online business. You've decided you're tired of chasing paper bills and it's time to address your chronic illness, spend time with grandchildren, etc. Whatever your motive is for choosing a Laptop Entrepreneur lifestyle, everyone loves **owning** their schedule rather than having someone up top set it for you.

3 Traits that Make a Successful Laptop Entrepreneur

Now that we've established why people are choosing to live a Laptop Entrepreneur lifestyle, it's important to see if you have what it takes. This lifestyle isn't for everyone - especially if you're planning on operating a virtual business which is the most demanding Laptop Entrepreneur structure. But, you'll likely thrive if you've got the following traits:

You Get Things Done On Time. It's bad enough to turn something in late when working at a traditional job, but it's ten times worse when you're working online. Imagine things from an employer's perspective: they've trusted you to get your work done from home, and now you're slacking off. How will they be able to contact you or get a refund? These are the concerns that run through your clients' minds when working from home and blowing them off. Or, imagine you're freelancing and turned in a project a week late - it's hard enough to trust people in person, let alone online. That client may decide not to work with you again or ask for a refund. If you're going to start working online, you need to be on top of your schedule and get things done when you say you will in order to earn and maintain trust.

You're Organized. Organization is a valuable trait in traditional 9 to 5 in-person jobs, but even more so online. You may have multiple clients to juggle. You may be working with multiple products or multiple blogs. You need to keep all of the information straight. If you're the type of person that has a junk drawer full of old papers and random things, chances are you need to work on developing better organization strategies before you take on working from home where managing a virtual file cabinet (e.g. your computer files, Google Drive, etc.) can be complex and become messy quickly.

You're Responsible. Not only are you responsible for producing quality work that's equal to, or better, than what you'd produce at a traditional job, you're also responsible for your own actions. When you're on your own creating a website, monetizing your blog, or researching properties to rent on Airbnb, nobody is responsible for the success or failure of your business but you. You have no employer to fall back on, no colleagues to blame. If you can bear the responsibility of being fully autonomous online, then being a laptop entrepreneur's an option for you.

You Have a Quiet, Distraction Free Workplace. Since you likely chose to become a Laptop Entrepreneur in the first place to improve your work-life balance, don't ruin it by working in a chaotic environment. If you don't have time to set aside to focus on your business or duties as a freelancer or employer, it's not going to work for you in the long-run. To help improve your work-life balance, try to set up an office or designated desk that you only use for distraction-free work. Eventually, you will begin to associate that place with work; not relaxing or play-time with the kids, etc. And that's super important. When you're in work mode, you want to be in full-on work mode. This helps you accomplish more and allows you to completely forget about work when you're off the clock so you can focus on more important pursuits.

You Have WiFi (No Matter Where You Are). Just because you're traveling, you have no excuses to not work. You have to be just as disciplined as if you were working from home. Want to head out to the full moon party on the beach in Thailand? That's probably not a wise idea if you've got a big assignment due the next day! When you're traveling, be sure to seek out Airbnbs, hostels, apartments and hotels with WiFi. In many places around the world, it's not uncommon to not have wifi. Do your homework before booking, and try to find internet cafes nearby just in case.

You Can Read and Research Before Jumping Into Things. You can really damage yourself if you're the type of person to jump into things without due diligence - both financially and in terms of your time. If you decide to create a blog on giraffes, for example, because it interests you...you may be screwing yourself in the future. It may take you a few months to create the content, build the website, collect amazing pictures of giraffes only to find that there are no monetization strategies around your giraffe niche. How do you avoid this? Research! Find out if there's demand and a gap in the market - if there is, you have a potential virtual business.

You're Capable of Filing Your Own Taxes. If you're working for your regular employer but have negotiated an online working contract, this isn't an issue for you. But, if you're freelacincing or running your own business online, you'll need to pay taxes on your own. The last thing you want are tax collectors breathing down your neck! This means saving for your retirement and contributing to healthcare on your own, too. With a little research (or investment in tax consulting), you can ensure your tax situation is squared away to avoid future headaches.

You're Innovative. Being a laptop entrepreneur often involves thinking outside of the box. You're limited to working with digital products and services, or coming up with clever strategies to manage to sell physical products without a physical storefront. That takes some major problem solving skills and innovation. If you're creative and the type of person to find solutions - no matter what - you'd be a great candidate for freelancing or running a virtual business.

Now that we've uncovered why more and more are choosing to live a Laptop Entrepreneur lifestyle and what it takes to start working online, I'm going to cover the four main structures of making money online. This isn't an exhaustive, step-by-step guide, but should give you the general idea - and inspiration - to get started. Whether you decide to work with your current company online, freelance or create a virtual business, you'll have a framework to get started. I'll discuss the pros and cons of each option so you know which is right for you. Keep reading to find out how you can fatten your wallet and live with less stress by implementing one of the four Laptop Entrepreneur models!

4 Common Laptop Entrepreneur Business Models

Many are choosing to ditch traditional work settings, opting to work online for more freedom in their schedules. In general, there are four models that shape the digital workforce. As we've covered, there are a variety of reasons for this shift in the workplace that range from being able to sleep in and setting one's own hours, to not having to commute to work, to being able to spend more time with family. When you pursue one of these four strategies, you'll see that there are certain advantages and disadvantages to each method. I've broken all of that down for you after several hours of research, as well as personal experience. I believe there's a place for everyone in the digital marketplace, and the more people that enter, the more digital positions will be created. It's a win-win situation for all involved! Working online expands the novel digital workforce frontier, which stimulates the economy, and clearly has several advantages for the individuals who choose to work from home. With that being said, let's explore the four main models of making money online that are actionable and produce real results.

In summary, Laptop Entrepreneurism can be broken into four main groups:

1. Remote Work Contract

Working at home rather than the office with your current employer to allow more schedule flexibility and personal freedom. This may be an option that's already offered, or you may have to pitch the idea to your current employer. This is especially adapted for jobs that can be done independently, like accounting, secretarial work, copywriting, and marketing.

2. Using a Freelancing Platform

Selling your services to ready-to-order buyers online. I'll cover two of the most popular freelancing platforms, Upwork and Fiverr, in depth. You'll see that, while these platforms do take a percentage of your earnings, many like how easy it is to set up their profile and start making money almost instantly. However, many more find that the rates are low and many of the buyers on these websites are looking to cut corners, thus paying little and expecting a lot.

3. Working Independently as a Freelancer

How you can leverage your own website or a professional platform like LinkedIn to reel in clients and make money with your digital services. While this requires more work to start (namely creating the website and generating leads), with the right system and a little SEO for your website, you can gain several clients to work with on a consistent basis. Best of all: you set your own rates and there's nobody to take a percentage of your earnings!

4. Operating a Virtual Business

Unlike the other three options, running your own eBusiness can be fully passive i.e. you're not trading your time for money, but rather you're selling a product for money instead. I'll cover the following options: dropshipping, blogging, affiliate marketing, selling products (both physical and digital) and renting property. While other strategies do exist (such as investing in the stock market), these are the ones that are most common and familiar to me. Best of all, it's probably not as hard as you think and can earn you thousands - or even millions!

Each option bears a different amount of personal responsibility and risk, which I'll explain further. Keep in mind, all of these strategies are actionable and realistic. There are many other guides out there that create unrealistic expectations like you can become a millionaire filling out surveys from home online (seriously - there are 7 billion people in the world. Nobody's opinion is that important!) or that you can make $1,000,000 each year blogging just like them (the problem is: A. They have a unique skill set that most people don't have, which is why most others will fail. For example, not everyone will make $10,000 a month in ebook sales, far above the average. Many, however, will take their individual success and pretend that others are capable of doing the same, when in fact, not everyone is cut out to write an ebook nonetheless market it or B. They haven't actually made as much money as they claim and are selling pipe dreams).

The advice and strategies I offer are real and fool-proof. If you have a profitable skill or have found a valuable product to sell in a niche market, you will make money - if you put in the effort. It's not a question of **if** you will make money, it's a question of **how much** will you make. For some of you, you'll only make a few hundred dollars each month (or potentially even less if you don't do your research). For others, you'll go off and make millions. The problem is that most people aren't willing to put in the effort and instead prefer the traditional route of making money, clocking in at a 9 to 5 job, since it's easy and safe. But taking the road less traveled and implementing one of these four techniques can lead to both personal and financial freedom.

With all that being said, let's take a look at the ways to make money from the comfort of your own home - or beachfront bungalow somewhere abroad!

5 Remote Work Contracts

Employers that allow employees the opportunity to work from home are becoming more and more common. As Millenials mature in the marketplace, many are choosing to pursue a virtual route rather than the typical face-to-face business model. The option to move from the office to your own home is great for those looking for stability or for those who'd like to give the Laptop Entrepreneur lifestyle a try without fully investing (both in terms or time and money. The other options are a bit more entailed and don't guarantee you a set salary as your current career probably does). Quite a few companies are already jumping on this trend, allowing employees to work virtually on Fridays. This is becoming quite popular among programming companies, as I've already mentioned. Additionally, some businesses are even allowing employees to work entirely virtually. The catch? You just need to come to a few meetings to make sure everyone's on the same page. You may be expected to meet in-person on a monthly, quarterly or even yearly basis (this presents its own unique set of pros and cons, which I'll discuss later). There are even some companies that operate entirely online, too. Everything from hiring to management to communication takes place online, usually with the help of Skype or Google Hangouts to ensure the team stays up to speed. While this practice isn't as typical, it's becoming more commonplace. More and more businesses are deciding to operate on a fully-remote basis.

When searching for remote work, you just need to take a look at LinkedIn or Indeed.com; you'll notice many companies are offering jobs that can be done entirely online. From positions in sales, to content management, to software engineering. There's a slice of Digital Nomad pie for everyone who has the right skill set for the online workplace.

Pros of Remote Work Contracts

Working virtually via a remote work contract is becoming more in demand by employees since it allows them to earn the same salary while working entirely online. Trading in the cubicle for the home office is a safer option for those looking for job security and a stable income while working as a Laptop Entrepreneur. It's essentially the same as working in an office - the only thing that's changed is the environment. Unlike working independently as a freelance worker (two of the other four work from home options), having an employer that entrusts you to work online allows you to earn a stable income that's not always guaranteed as a freelance contract worker (which is often on a project-basis or short-term duration). If you want an income that's guaranteed, choosing to go remote with your current workplace is the best option for you.

On top of the stable salary, you'll also likely receive benefits. Since contract workers or freelancers aren't considered employees, accessing benefits is enjoyed uniquely by virtual employees. Things that can be a part of your working contract include: medical and dental insurance, vision, retirement savings accounts, reimbursement for travel expenses and other benefits agreed upon in the contract. This is advantageous when compared to working as a freelancer online on a per-project basis. Not having to foot the bill when visiting the doctor or paying for airfare to meet face-to-face is clearly the more ideal situation!

Since you're considered an employee, this also makes filing taxes a lot easier, too. Working as a freelancer online means you're operating your own business (i.e. you have to pay taxes on the money you've earned). This becomes tricky and may involve hiring an accountant or paying someone to file taxes for you. Contrastingly, when working online for an employer, taxation is likely taken care of automatically via social security deductions government withholdings as well as pensions, Social Security, and other savings plans. This saves your time and the headache of having to file taxes on your own as a sole proprietor or corporation.

And the good news is: should you decide the remote lifestyle isn't for you, you can always choose to resume working in a traditional office setting. This option is great for those with cold feet, allowing a taste of the Laptop Entrepreneur lifestyle without fully investing in it and quitting your stable job. Since you'll likely already have a face-to-face job when choosing this option, transitioning to the digital landscape is easy. And, you'll likely always have the option to return back to your cubicle if you decide working online isn't for you.

Cons of Remote Work Contracts

While the benefits of working online with a remote work contract are endless, there are some negative aspects that should be considered. One of the biggest issues remote contract workers face is limited income potential (whether they realize it or not). Many choose to get into the Laptop Entrepreneur lifestyle in order to make exponential income (usually passive income) from anywhere in the world. This means making money for yourself - not for your boss. It takes a hard-working, self-motivated person to become a Laptop Entrepreneur that operates a virtual business. While you can be self-motivated and hard-working while working for a boss, you're still severely limited in what you can do and how much you can make. Being paid a salary means your income is stagnant - you may receive a bonus here and there, but your income will never increase much (and, naturally, most Laptop Entrepreneurs work for themselves hope their income fluctuates in an upward fashion!). Working independently online - either operating your business virtually or working as an independent freelancer - allows you to maximize your income potential, whereas a remote contract limits your income to your current salary.

Another factor to consider is that when you work for another person or business, you have less time to devote to creating your own business. Digital Nomads are entrepreneurial in nature - when working on a remote contract, you have less time to devote to developing your own virtual business and skillset. Each hour spent working for another means less time focusing on carving your own path in the digital landscape. Plus, it can be draining to put in a full 40 hour work week and then try to fit in time to make your own money online. It'll be hard to find the creative energy needed to develop your own products or services for yourself if working for someone else full-time! There are plenty of opportunities to create income online - when working for someone else, you have less opportunity to claim your own stake in the digital marketplace.

Working for someone else means giving up certain freedoms, too. While contracts can vary, you can expect your remote work contract to lay out a minimum number of hours to be worked each week. That means you can't plan around your own schedule - you still have to work a set amount of hours that's not determined by you, but rather your employer and their timezone. This is different from working online independently. When working online as an independent freelancer or operating a virtual business, you have full control over when you work. And since you may be traveling as a Digital Nomad, you will have to adjust your schedule around your employer's time. Clearly, this can be a problem for someone living halfway around the world from their employer. This means you don't entirely own your schedule - your life and your routine must revolve around that of your employer still;.

While this may not be a problem for those who live within or near the same time zone, those who are a bit more East or West may have difficulties keeping up with their employer's schedule.

The Bottom Line

While many may get into the Laptop Entrepreneur lifestyle to make money online their own way, some may choose the safer route: simply switching from a traditional office setting to a digital one. Of course, the transition would be much smoother if this is something your current company is already offering. If not, you can always pitch the idea or explore other employment opportunities to find something more flexible and technologically-forward.

PROS

- Stable work & income
- May have employee benefits (i.e. medical & dental insurance, travel reimbursement)
- Option to revert back to a traditional office setting
- Straight-forward taxation

CONS

- Limited income potential (i.e. can't set own working rate, scale business, create passive income, etc.)
- Less time to develop personal business & skills
- Less scheduling flexibility

6 Using a Freelancing Platform

When trying to break into the digital freelancing field, many find themselves creating profiles on freelancing platforms such as UpWork, Guru, Freelancer and Fiverr. The allure of having a multitude of interested clients at freelancers' fingertips draws newbies in. Little do they know, however, using freelancing platforms may be one of the *least profitable* ways to generate income online. The ease of profile creation and the accessibility to thousands of shoppers looking to hire freelancers makes this an appealing option for many trying to make a living online. However, the convenience comes with significant disadvantages as well; namely the steep cuts into your paycheck freelancing platforms take.

Working as a freelancer online via a platform is still a very popular option, however, and can even make you hundreds of thousands of dollars each year. The ease of not having to generate leads keeps many freelancers hooked to the platform without having to spend a lot of time creating a website and finding clients interested in your services. Using freelancing platforms can be a consistent, user-friendly way of generating income online. Best of all, there are a variety of fields freelancers can choose from. Whether pursuing something niche like MailChimp email campaigns for beauty products, or pursuing something as wide as programming, there's something for everyone when looking for work online via platforms. Using freelance platforms often serves as a first step when pursuing a virtual career and can work towards building your portfolio for future opportunities.

Pros of Using a Freelance Platform

Using a freelance platform is similar to using a point-and-shoot camera (like the one on your cellphone). Instead of having to adjust the aperture and focus, everything is done automatically by machine. Similarly, with freelancing platforms, you just upload your profile highlighting your valuable, in-demand skillset and *voila* - you should have buyers coming in. Of course, that's an oversimplification - you do need to put in a bit more effort than that. But the point is, shoppers specifically go to freelance platforms like Fiverr, Upwork and Guru with the intention of buying services from someone. The hard part is balancing the right price point given the competition and your skillset. Once you've found your niche, it's easy to build a strong portfolio, and therefore your reputation and rating, which leads to more buyers.

Setting up a profile on a freelance platform can be done in minutes. They offer user-friendly interfaces, making it easy to create a catchy description of your services and display your portfolio beautifully. On Fiverr, for example, there are a few sections that you need to fill out when creating a "gig" (a service that you sell on the marketplace). You need to select the appropriate categories that define your gig, create a title that captures attention and contains important keywords, write an enticing description, set your pricing strategy (Fiverr offers three main packages: Basic, Standard and Premium), add a video or picture, and that's it! Upwork operates a bit differently. While you do need to create a profile and catchy description, Upwork makes it more buyer-focused. What I mean by that is you need to come to the buyer, rather than the other way around. On Fiverr the buyer shops around for you; on Upwork, you shop for the buyer. While it can be tedious having to send a cover letter each time you apply for a job on Upwork, the job offers tend to be on an ongoing basis and pay higher rates than on Fiverr. Upwork requires you to spend *connects* which are virtual coins used to apply for jobs. Prior to May 2019, each freelancer would get 30 connects every month with each job proposal costing 2 connects (so, 15 job proposals total per month for free). You had the option to spend money to purchase *connects* if you ran out of the 30, or you could buy into a premium plan which offers more connects, in addition to other benefits. Now, the freelancing platform has taken things a bit too far as some of its users would say. Connects are no longer free and can range from 1 to 6 connects for each job proposal. Each connect costs $0.15. If you apply to a job that requires 6 connects, that translates into having to pay $0.90 just to apply to a job. While this can be annoying for some users and has pushed them to migrate off the platform, others have chosen to stay due to consistent work and more agreeable clients to work with than other platforms or freelancing independently.

Another benefit of using a freelancing platform is headache-free payments from clients. There's no need to send out invoices, and no need to follow-up with clients to ensure they've paid the money they owe you. On Fiverr, the buyer purchases the gig with the reassurance that they can receive their money back if they're not satisfied. Upwork provides an even better, more secure system. All funds are put into escrow, meaning the buyer pays for the funds and they are set aside until the job or "milestone" (a smaller task within the larger project) is complete. Additionally, if you work on an hourly contractual basis, your funds are guaranteed when using Upwork's Hour Tracker app. The app takes screenshots of your computer at random while you run the clock on your employer. When you opt-in to the Hour Tracker app, you are guaranteed your funds in escrow since you have proof that you've worked the hours claimed (as opposed to entering the hours you've worked manually; in that case you're not guaranteed that the employer will pay you).

One other thing that Laptop Entrepreneurs like about using freelancer platforms is the ease of accessing and withdrawing funds. With the click of a button, you can withdraw the money you've earned to PayPal or directly to your bank after going through a few security steps to confirm your account. Some freelance platforms offer this service for free (i.e. Upwork) while others, like Fiverr, charge a $1 withdrawal fee (which has been removed recently - there is now no fee to withdraw to PayPal on Fiverr as of writing this). Additionally, paying taxes is a lot easier with the help of freelancing platforms than having to generate income reports on your own. There's nothing to enter into a spreadsheet or QuickBooks; it's all taken care of for you. Each transaction, along with the date and order number are recorded in a file, allowing you to keep track of your income on one convenient sheet. Since there are fees that these freelancing platforms take from your earnings (which I'll cover in the 'cons') there is one positive point to the high percentage deduction (or, at least with Upwork): it's 100% tax-deductible. You can write off any fees you incur on Upwork, lowering the amount you have to pay when it's time to file taxes.

Cons of Using a Freelance Platform

As mentioned, one of the most obvious drawbacks of using a freelance platform is having to give up a (hefty) portion of your income in fees. Fiverr and Upwork both withhold the same amount of your earnings: 20% (although Upwork operates on a different scheme. After reaching certain thresholds with a client, the percentage that they take is reduced). For many freelancers, that percentage is way too high, which is why they skip the middleman and create their own businesses, working independently as freelancers instead. It may be harder to gather clients, but they rely on the reputation of their high-quality work and personal branding to get them stable clients. To put the 20% fee in perspective, for every $1000 you charge a client, you'll only get $800. $200 of your hard-earned money goes completely out the window (and, with Fiverr, this amount isn't tax deductible!). While freelancing platform proponents argue that it still pays off to use their platforms (afterall, they are saving you time finding clients, marketing resources, etc.) many are pushed away by the high fees and strict rules, as well as demanding buyers on the platforms.

Upwork

Upwork's history started not as a single company, but two. In 2015, Elance and oDesk joined together to become Upwork (prior, in 2013 they were known as Eland-oDesk). Now, the website hosts 12 million registered freelancers, and the competition is stiff: there are only five million registered clients. If you do the math, that works out to be about a two to one ratio of workers to employers. And not every client posts a job. In fact, there are only 3 million jobs posted each year, meaning there's only one job for every four job-seekers on the platform. While the competition is tough - especially when competing with people who live in low cost of living countries that can charge lower rates - if you're good at what you do, there's always room in the market for you. You can find jobs that are paid by the hour or one time fee jobs. Additionally, you can filter jobs by hourly pay, experience level, and contract length.

If you're the type of person that doesn't like job applications, Upwork isn't for you, however. Unlike Fiverr, where you can create gigs that are listed automatically, you have to apply to each and every job (unless by some miracle you're discovered and invited to apply to a job by a client). That means sifting through your portfolio to find similar projects you've completed, writing out a cover letter (which, to improve your chances of being selected must be unique for each and every listing), and answering any additional questions the client may ask. And guess what? Even after all that work, it's still not guaranteed that the client will select you. And if you're not careful, you can burn through your *connects* (i.e. your money) fast just by applying to jobs.

But Upwork's not all that bad - if it were, there wouldn't be millions of freelancers who've signed up to use the platform. You can make money; although, you'll have to submit several applications and be willing to accept Upwork's high fees.

Upwork's Freelance Service Fees

When you earn money on Upwork, you're, "charged a sliding fee based on your lifetime billings." This means that the more money you make with a client, the lower the percentage fee you're charged. And, it applies for all contracts with the same client - whether they're from a year ago or last week. The money that you earn with each client accumulates, helping you to reach lower fees.

Upworks fee schedule for freelancers:

- $0-$500: **20%**
- $500.01-$10,000: **10%**
- $10,000.01 or more: **5%**

Here's an example: let's say you have worked with a client on a project for $800 (fixed rate or hourly - it doesn't matter. The fee schedule applies to both types of freelancing contracts). Upwork would take 20% of the first $500 (which would be $100), and then 10% of the remaining $300 (which would be $30). In total, you'd be charged $130 and be left with $670 (before taxes, of course). Compared to other freelancing platforms like Fiverr, using Upwork would be advantageous in this scenario (since you'd be left with more of your hard-earned money).

One other thing you may be wondering is: when will you get paid? Unfortunately, it's not instantaneous for hourly contracts. You must submit all of your hours by Monday (if using the manual hour tracker method). If using the Hour Tracker app from Upwork, it's all taken care of for you. Then, the employer has five days (until Friday) to dispute the hours. If everything is fine, you'll get paid on Wednesday.

In summary, here's how Hourly Contracts work:

Monday to Sunday (Week 1) This is when you work - either using the Hour Tracking App or putting in the hours manually.

Monday (Week 2): The hours are finalized on Monday for the previous work week. If tracking your hours manually, be sure to submit your hours by this time.

Friday (Week 2): If everything's clear, the employer will approve your working hours by this time. This usually isn't a problem, especially when using the Hour Tracking App where payments are guaranteed.

Wednesday (Week 3): Upwork makes your funds available. You can withdraw to PayPal or your bank instantly.

The fees Upwork takes out of your earnings isn't the only thing to consider, however. You'll also be charged when you use *connects* to apply for contract work. That means it actually **costs** you money to apply for jobs. And as of May 2019, you're not given free connects each month (which was the case before). Each job costs between one and six connects, and since you have to purchase connects at $0.15, that means every time you apply for a job, it'll cost you between $0.15 and $0.90! However, according to Upwork, freelancers usually spend less than $5 each month applying to jobs. Why did Upwork start charging its freelancers to apply to jobs? Their strategy is to reduce the number of job applications from freelancers so that clients can have a more select, high-quality batch of applicants, rather than receive generic applications *en masse* from freelancers.

If you still think it's worth it to use Upwork - the world's largest freelancing marketplace - you can signup at Upwork.com. It's fast and easy to fill out your profile, sift through jobs and upload work to your portfolio. Be sure to research keywords and write strong, convincing copy on your profile to increase the chances you're selected (or discovered) by clients.

Fiverr

Fiverr is another popular freelancing marketplace online. The Israel-based company was started in 2010 allowing sellers to price their services at just $5. In 2013, Fiverr started allowing freelancers to charge more than $5 for their services. Since then, the website has grown tremendously and is mainly dominated by young adults looking to live the Laptop Entrepreneur lifestyle. Unfortunately, being fully "free" as most people want to be as Laptop Entrepreneurs is very difficult when suing Fiverr. Fiverr has been criticised by many for being very restrictive and crashing the freelancing marketplace wages. While Upwork does require its freelancers to respond quickly to clients in order to be successful on the platform, Fiverr is much more strict. You are expected to reply to messages as quickly as possible - from buyers all over the world - so that your gigs can rank higher on the marketplace. This means if someone messages you at 1:00 am in China and you don't respond until 9:00 am, your response time was 8 hours. Obviously, you can't answer messages in your sleep, so many freelancers (myself included) found themselves checking Fiverr messages first thing in the morning and last thing at night to ensure the response time was fast enough.

Another thing that many freelancers find annoying about Fiverr is the high percentage fee. Unlike Upwork's fee schedule, which diminished as you make more money with a client, Fiverr's fee is always

20%. It doesn't matter if you make $10 or $1,000 with a client - you'll be paying 20% to Fiverr no matter what! And, it's not tax deductible either. On top of that, Fiverr has earned itself a reputation for being a marketplace for cheap work. And by cheap, I don't mean low-cost but low-quality. In 2014, Fiverr ran a campaign on Facebook stating, "You're paying too much for design," which angered many freelancers. Many felt that Fiverr was driving the prices for digital services down. Design, writing, programming and any other online service takes time and usually expertise - when Fiverr published this campaign, many found that they were putting in a lot of time trying to meet their clients' demands while being forced to price their work below its value to stay competitive.

Since Fiverr took this low cost approach, many are choosing to skip this platform. In fact, freelancers and clients alike are choosing to abandon this platform since both parties usually become disappointed. Freelancers are disappointed in undercharging for their services (and then having to pay out 20% to Fiverr) while buyers are usually disappointed with the low-quality work they often get as many freelancers cut corners to deliver quickly and cheaply.

But there are two advantages to using Fiverr: the first is you get paid to grow your portfolio. Unlike working for free to try your hand at new skills, you'll get paid to put your skills to the test. If you took a course on Udemy on web design, for example, it could be strategic for you to create a "Gig" (service listing on Fiverr) so that you can practice and gain experience. The second advantage is that clients shop for your services. All you need to do is create your "Gigs", add some photos and a description, research keywords, and you're set! There's no need to apply to jobs as there is on Upwork. You simply add your gigs to the marketplace and wait for buyers to find you.

Fiverr's Payment Structure for Freelancers

Unlike Upwork, Fiverr's payment structure is a lot more straight-forward. It is also, however, more time-consuming (meaning you have to wait longer for the funds to clear before you can withdraw them). As you know, Fiverr takes 20%. When you finish a project and the buyer accepts (or, if the buyer doesn't accept your delivery, it's automatically cleared after 72 hours of submitting the project) you must wait 14 days in order for the funds to clear. Once the funds are cleared, you can withdraw to your bank or PayPal.

In summary, getting paid on Fiverr works like this:

Buyer Accepts or Rejects. Once you've finished a project, you'll upload your work for the buyer to approve or reject. Keep in mind that since reviews are extremely important on Fiverr (and buyers know this) you may run into difficult buyers who demand you do things beyond what was offered...or else. And that "or else" means they'll give you a bad review, which lowers the amount of work you get. So basically, you're a slave for some of these buyers. Oh, and if you want to cancel an order? Good luck! You can't cancel a gig from your end without damaging your "Cancelation Rate," so you'll have to ask the buyer to do that for you. It can be a hectic and complicated process.

20% Fee. After the buyer accepts your work, or the 72 hours have passed after you submit the project, you'll finally get your money! Except...you have to wait two weeks. And of course, as I've mentioned multiple times, you'll need to accept the fact that 20% of your money goes out the window.

2 Week Clearance. Before you can access your funds, you need to wait two weeks. When I was using Fiverr, I'd usually withdraw my funds once every two weeks or every month (especially when they were charging $1 to withdraw to PayPal).

The Bottom Line

You can absolutely make money using freelancing platforms; the question is: are you willing to sacrifice some of your profits and are you willing to give up your freedom (i.e. you must reply quickly and are forced to work with certain clients, even if you don't want to). If so, a freelancing platform like Fiverr and Upwork may be right for you. It can be a great way to encounter eager buyers without having to go through the laborious task of creating your own website and finding your own leads.

PROS

- Convenient source of buyers
- Low barrier to entry (no website, branding, finding clients, etc.)
- User-friendly interface
- Payments in escrow, easily withdrawable to a bank or paypal
- Automatically generated income reports to file tax easily
- Tax deductible expenses (just for Upwork)

CONS

- Fees for withdrawing funds and clearance and high fees (around 20%)
- You're not a person; you're a service
- Little flexibility
- Less freedom to reject difficult clients
- Lowered income due to internation- alization ("race to the bottom")

7 Working Independently as a Freelancer

For freelancers with a bit more experience under their belt and drive to make more money, working for yourself (i.e. without a freelancing platform) is the best option. But a word of caution: it isn't as "turn-key". In fact, you're going to need to put in a reasonable amount of upfront work before you start seeing any results. This usually entails creating your own website (with WordPress typically). Which is yet another skill to learn. However, if you'd rather spend a bit of cash, you can always hire somebody else to build it for you. You'll also need to leverage your network on LinkedIn (which requires a complete profile, many connections, keyword research, and more) and finding a way to accept and record payment transactions (one of the most common is with PayPal, while others with a more robust website may decide to use a payment platform via WooCommerce; an extension on WordPress).

Whether you've worked for a freelancing platform and are fed up with their fragile rules and cuts into your profit, or are going at freelancing online for the first time, you'll likely start making more money than using a freelancing platform. Many buyers are realizing you're not going to get much with $5; especially from freelancing platforms that treat their work supply like cattle, waiting for the next batch to be churned out. Additionally, another highlight of paving your own road is that when you're on your own website it's you alone who shines. You're not pitted against people around the world who can live off of $5 a day (i.e. there's less competition). When someone lands on your website the spotlight is entirely on you - it's up to your copy, portfolio and expertise to convince buyers to stick around.

Pros of Working Independently as a Freelancer

As mentioned, when you work online as a freelancer, you have the entire spotlight on yourself. This isn't time to play it shy; let buyers know why they should pick you. Include past work examples and explain why you do what you do best. When you get an inquiry, provide value and ensure your response is specific to their situation. This ensures that buyers move forward with you and not the other sellers surrounding your listing (like on Fiverr, for example). Buyers don't have to sort through dozens of results for the same task they're looking for when they land on your website or LinkedIn. While they may have to search through multiple search engine result pages, they're at least not bombarded with videos and images from all kinds of different sellers at all different price points.

Not only can you focus more on yourself and the value you can bring to potential clients, you can also set your own rules. As previously discussed, when you're on Fiverr and Upwork you don't have full control. Rather, you must act in accordance with their Terms of Service agreement which can be quite restrictive. At least when you're working online as an independent freelancer, you don't have the clock constantly ticking in the back of your head as you do on Fiverr. With Fiverr, sellers are expected to respond as possible to all requests. And if not? The algorithm boots your gig ranking down. Contrastingly, when you're out there on your own in Laptop Entrepreneur land carving out your territory as an independent freelancer, you can reply when you want to and work with whoever you wish.

This isn't to say you should take your time when replying, but it does mean that your stress load will be greatly reduced. If you wake up in the middle of the night, your first thought shouldn't be "oh jeez, I should check my Fiverr to see who I need to respond to". When you're working independently, you will likely attract non "bargain buyers" who understand you need sleep and probably have other duties and projects you're working on. Also, they can't hold your review hostage which is a huge plus.

That's another insider secret to working online as an independent freelancer; you can refuse clients. Just because someone is offering money doesn't mean you have to accept. Many buyers on freelancing platforms act like you've sold them your soul and therefore you must do as they say...if not, be prepared for a 1-star review. Contrastingly, that's not the case when you're working online for yourself. While some online freelancers do have review systems in place and testimonials (which likely increase buyer activity since consumers are looking for social proof - especially on an online context), you don't have to bend over backwards just to get reviews. You build your reputation based on the **value** you provide clients; not on how much you're willing to bend over for bargain buyers.

Cons of Working Independently as a Freelancer

The cons of working online as a freelancer are less than the pros, but you still have some negative aspects you need to consider before investing yourself in this method. For starters, you need to realize there's still lots of competition online (even if you're not pitted against other freelancers side-by-side as you are on freelancing platforms). But, anyone who understands basic economics understands there's a market for everything. The market will sort you out. If you're a recently graduated student with little experience and no major projects under your name, it's no surprise you can't command top-dollar projects. But, if you're good at what you do, have natural talent and leverage your network, nothing's impossible. You can charge the most for your work. It all depends on you and your skill level, as well as reputation. That's one thing some people can struggle with when freelancing independently; there's an ever-increasing level of competition. But, fortunately, the market has a variety of dynamics to sort the situation out itself. Think of it like selling fruit at a market. You have geographic factors: those who are in the richer parts of town will likely charge a higher price, simply based on their location. Then, you have quality factors; those who sell, brighter, more nutrient-dense produce free of harmful pesticides can sell for a higher price than those selling produce that's been sprayed with RoundUp ("Glyphosate"), for example. Then, you have sellers who are more friendly and have established relationships with their patrons. They are likely to get repeat business and can charge more.

That is, in essence, how the marketplace works for freelancers. You need to carve out your territory as a figurative fruit seller. This process can be intimidating for many people since there may be so many other people doing what you're doing. That's why niches are important: when everyone is selling kiwis, sell bananas. When everyone is focusing on quality, opt for selling a higher quantity at a lower price point. Overall, getting into the "groove" of the marketplace and finding a strategy can be a challenge for some people, but many still find success working online.

Another downfall is that you must file your taxes all on your own. Depending on the jurisdiction you belong to, this can be complicated - especially when traveling the world as a digital nomad. Complicated questions may arise, like: where do you pay your taxes as a U.S. citizen who is currently based in Indonesia but made most of his or her digital content in Thailand. In summary, navigating taxation as an independent freelancer can be difficult to manage (but very doable!). Many are able to travel the world, taking advantage of Double Taxation treaties and programs like the Estonia eResidency to make paying taxes easier.

Paying taxes isn't the only hard part of being a successful freelancer online. Channeling one's entrepreneurial spirit can also be a challenge for those trying to sell their digital services online. Traditional business owners have the advantage of having real objects, real places, real face-to-face interactions. Independent freelancers, on the other hand, must navigate their own path - all online. This can be exceptionally hard - it's hard enough to be an entrepreneur and follow your own path in person, but it can be even harder when dealing with non-physical products and a non-physical environment. You really have to ensure your clients trust you and express your value clearly and quickly so that buyers don't click away.

Another disadvantage to being an independent freelancer is that you're still trading your time for money. Unlike operating a business online, you're still putting in your efforts for money, rather than selling a product or service (not carried out by you) for money. Despite the fact that being a freelancer isn't a passive income strategy, it's still a great way to make an active income.

In-Demand, High Paying Freelance Skills

Not sure where to start? Here are some high-demand (and high-paying!) freelancing skills:

Programming and Software Development
If you're "techy" this is for you! You can go to school and study something like Computer Science, but many developers and programmers have taught themselves. This is a field that's in high-demand, and of course, commands a high salary!

Graphic Design
Graphic design is, not surprisingly, one of the most popular freelancing fields. While the market is saturated, you can make a name for yourself

- if you're creative and talented. If you're artistic and want to help brands tell their stories, this is for you.

Web Design and Development

If you're skilled in WordPress, or making websites from scratch, your best bet may be to pursue web design. While it may seem intimidating at first, it's easy once you get the hang of it. You can teach yourself with an e-course on Udemy or by lots and lots of reading tutorials online.

Video Editing

Since it's so time-consuming and requires a skillful eye to edit videos, this is something that's commonly outsourced to freelancers. Want to help top YouTubers grow their channels with awesome editing? Or, maybe you want to edit videos for professionals to add to their website. If you do, you can try to pursue video editing.

Social Media Management

Social media isn't just for fun more; companies can make big bucks with a strong social media presence. Social media helps engage current customers and lets businesses reach new audiences. It seems easy but requires a balance between strong copywriting and graphic design.

Content Marketing and SEO

(Hey, that's what I do! If you're interested in taking your online presence to the next level - meaning more sales and visits - contact me at RyanScottSEO.com). Content marketing is something that almost anyone can do - but that doesn't mean they do it well! You need to be a skilled writer, up to date with the latest SEO best-practices and know how to write catchy, clickable headlines. If you think you have what it takes, try getting clients for content marketing. If not, you can always hire me!

While it's great working in these fields, the con is that you're still contributing your **time for money**. You can gain a big salary when working for yourself online but it's still a time for money situation instead of a product for money situation (which is more ideal). Even as a talented software engineer, the average salary is still $92,046 per year according to Glassdoor (as of February 4, 2020), when instead you can run a business online and make that same salary - but, passively. Or, with a little more effort and the right niche, you could make millions per year; all without having to work full time. But, that's not to say that all who run a business online make tons of money; in fact, many don't. But, one needs to ask themselves: would my life improve if I were making $30,000 annually in book sales (which requires maybe 1 hour of work per week after the initial writing process) versus making $70,000 as a freelance writer but working 30-40 hours per week. These are the types of questions you need to ask yourself before choosing a path. Some like the variation in projects and the stability working as a freelancer can bring, while others favor putting in the effort upfront in exchange for a (hopefully) lasting reward.

The Bottom Line

Working for yourself online is a great option for those looking to maximize their profit potential since there are no fees to pay (as you would on Fiverr and Upwork). While you can also make more money for yourself, you'll also be responsible for gaining your own clients and managing all aspects of your business (including keeping track of your invoices, expenses, filing taxes, etc.) If you're organized and have learned (or can learn) an in-demand skill, you have the potential of becoming a successful, independent freelancer.

PROS

- You can charge a fair rate
- Differentiate yourself (the spotlight is entirely on you/your portfolio, unlike freelancing platforms)
- Buyers know what they're looking for (usually)
- Schedule autonomy
- Ability to refuse clients
- Potential to scale business and/or outsource
- Higher income potential (no fees, less competition, etc.)

CONS

- Still trading time for money (unlike passive income strategies)
- More of a learning curve (have to create a website, advertise, market, etc.)
- Acquiring clients (requires networking and marketing)
- Start-up costs
- Must manage invoices
- More communication with buyers

8 Operating a Virtual Business

Who says starting a business needs to be done in person? It's 2020 - there's a world of opportunity available online! Laptop Entrepreneurs have been blazing new trails in the last few years, creating entirely digital business models online. There are varying degrees of what operating a "digital" business means (i.e. it's not entirely a digital business if you're dealing with physical products. For example, someone selling natural toothpaste on Etsy must still source the materials for the formula and packaging, create the product and manually ship the products). While other models are completely run online (i.e. those who sell ebooks, digital products, have an online digital agency and outsource the work to others, those who sell memberships and sponsored content, etc).

There are a variety of sub-models to choose from when using this Laptop Entrepreneur model. But, the point is, they are all feasible plans that can earn you real money - all from the comfort of your own home with your laptop. Keep in mind: making money online is not going to be easy. You'll need to put in tons of upfront work; that's much more difficult than filling out a few forms on Fiverr or leveraging your social media networks. Rather, you'll need to build things from the ground up with content creation, a new website, SEO, choose the right eCommerce platform to use (or create your own and sell directly from your website) and more. The waters become even more muddied if you choose to hire employees or you decide to outsource jobs to freelancers.

But with great complexity comes great reward. Since running an "in-person" business is hard enough, you'll realize that in many ways, running a virtual business can be easier. For starters, there is less competition online. Why? Starting a business is a bit more complex and involves a bit of "techy" skills. Not everyone is cut out to make money online. It takes a certain type of person to create a profitable business in the online world. One who is entrepreneurial, has a vision and is disciplined. Of all the options on the list, creating a virtual business has the highest earning potential. If you feel like you have a great idea, product or service offering, perhaps it's time that you leverage your skills and create your own website to start reeling in money. But, before you dig in, here are the pros and cons of creating and operating a digital business.

Types of Virtual Businesses

While there are a variety of ways to make money online, I'm going to walk you through some of the most successful types of businesses to operate online. This by no means is a guide to creating one of these businesses (which would take an entire ebook or e-course to thoroughly explain) but rather serves as a source of inspiration, capturing the idea and basic steps of the business model. Hopefully, you feel encouraged to explore the ideas further! I have included detailed resources for you to refer to for all of the types of virtual business in the following chapters.

Pros of Operating a Virtual Business

The best thing about running a virtual business is that you are free to make as much money as you want. You're not restricted by a fixed salary, you don't have an employer to ask for a raise, and you don't have to deal with percentage fees that cut into your profit (for the most part. Excluding the short-term rental business if you go through a property management company. But again - it's all passive and not active like on a freelancing platform!). You're completely in charge. While that's a big source of relief, having complete control over your business can be a stressor, too. When creating a business online, you are painting a blank canvas. While there are plenty of business models to emulate and others who have reached success, you have to design and implement your own strategy. Hopefully with the above virtual business models, you feel inspired to take your first step! Whether you choose something that's 100% online like selling a digital product, starting a blog, or choosing something more tangible like selling products or renting out your space, the key is that you're no longer trading your time for money, but have rather created a system that makes you money based on the value you've produced (i.e. a digital download, apartment you've redesigned for Airbnb guests, a cool product, etc).

To further emphasize: one of the biggest benefits of creating and implementing a virtual business model is that it's much more hands-off than working as a freelancer - for yourself or a platform - and working for a boss. Does that mean you won't have to put in up-front work? Or, that you won't ever have to tweak anything you've written or produced? No, absolutely not! It just means that those 40 hour weeks you've put in to creating your ebook, blog, or developing your winning product are working for you and lining your own pocket - not someone else's. Even when you work as a freelancer independently - say, as a web designer or software engineer - you're still making someone else's money. Freelancers are still simply cogs in a greater machine. As a virtual business owner, you run the show - it's your machine! That's the difference: you create a system selling products or services that you profit from - without trading your time for money.

If you're thinking of getting into the self-education business (like I am with this ebook) there's never been a better time than right now! Since the cost of tuition is so high and many are alarmed by the amount of political bias and indoctrination in Western nations, many are opting out of getting degrees and going to trade school - or, they skip formal higher education all together and look for resources (like e-courses) that help them learn a skill. That's where you come in! This is another advantage of running a digital business: you can create valuable information for others. Teach what you know best! And best of all, you don't have to worry about competition in the long-run. Skills and information are constantly evolving. For example, if you decide to create an ecourse on Azure (a programming language) someone else may learn from you and then go on to invent a programming language that's even more advanced and cutting-edge. That's how it works - people invest in your courses or ebooks to better their lives and create their own territory in the market - which then creates even more opportunities.

Another pro of running a digital business is you can delegate a lot of the work to others. Not a fan of paying your taxes? Don't do them - hire someone else instead. Hate writing SEO content? Great! Focus on product development (your strength) and leave that to someone specialized in search engine optimization (like me!). Since operating a virtual business is an entire system, you can choose which parts you want to engage in and which parts you want to hire others to do - especially once your business grows and matures. Overall, running a virtual business grants freedom and income generation that' not experienced by the other three digital nomad structures (but - it has its downsides, too).

Cons of Operating a Virtual Business

Running your own business online requires a lot of thinking outside of the box and research. Unlike traditional businesses which involve buying and selling goods or offering services in person, the online world is completely different i.e. it's a lot less straightforward. For example, you may not realize how important it is to grow an email list. Then, after you discover later it is important, you need to figure out the right optin campaign to run on your website (which can be hard to do on your own and expensive to outsource to someone else - especially if you don't have much money to invest in your business to begin with). In other words: there's a learning curve when it comes to creating and operating a virtual business.

And, when comparing running a virtual business to freelancing or working from home with an employer, it's scarier to make the leap (though, it's a lot more rewarding, too!). When you work for an employer or as a freelancer with regular clients, you gain a steady income. That's not the case with running a virtual business. There's always a chance it'll flop i.e. you won't make any money. Or worse: if you don't do your proper research and get too carried away with hiring people to create a website and run tons of paid ads, you may even lose hundreds of dollars. And you may not lose just money; you can also waste a lot of time writing blog posts, researching keywords and setting up social media accounts all for nothing. So, starting a business online runs a higher risk than starting a freelancing business in most cases.

Another thing to consider is that you won't have an employer. What's the implication? That means you'll have to file your own taxes (which can be tricky - especially if you're a Digital Nomad and travelling all over the world) and setting up your own retirement fund, paying your own medical expenses, etc. Additionally, you'll be required to set up a legal business as a sole proprietor (which is usually quick and easy, but means you're solely responsible for your business), or you can opt for creating a company (a Limited Liability Corporation - LLC) which comes with its own complications, pros and cons. Sometimes it's nice working for others since you don't have to deal with legal issues, aside from filing your taxes. When you're your own employer, everything's on your shoulders - which is incredibly freeing, but can also be daunting. Especially for new business owners.

The Bottom Line

Creating your own virtual business allows you to exchange value (i.e. either a physical product, virtual product or property) for money, rather than time for money. If you're willing to put in effort in the initial stages, this model may be best for you. Just be careful - it's less straight-forward than the other three options and requires more independence and problem solving skills. Another positive is that your profit potential is highest with this option. So if you're shooting for more money and, eventually, a system that you can operate hands-off, this is best for you.

PROS

- Unlimited income streams (dropshipping, blogging, etc.)
- More passive income strategies
- No shipping costs (if selling a digital product)
- Increasing demand for digital content, decreasing University demand
- Maximize profit potential

CONS

- Learning curve
- More intimidating
- No employee benefits
- More legal, logistics, etc. barriers

Dropshipping

For those of you who keep up with passive income strategies or ways to make money online, chances are you've heard of dropshipping before. In case you haven't: what is dropshipping? In essence, as a dropshipper you're responsible for creating the storefront and marking up the price of the product to cover expenses. The supplier (usually in China), on the other hand, handles the rest of the process. That means everything from creating the product to managing the inventory and getting it to the buyer on time is handled by the supplier (that's why you need to find someone you can trust. Cheaper isn't always better!). Dropshipping entails creating an attractive eCommerce website using **Shopify**, **BigCommerce**, or taking a more hands-on approach (i.e. more complicated, demanding a higher level and understanding of web design. If you don't have website building skills, it's best you opt for Shopify or BigCommerce as they're both beautifully designed, can be built easily and are beginner-friendly) with **WooCommerce** via WordPress. And of course, an attractive eCommerce website needs an attractive checkout system to accept payments. You'll need to set up a system to accept payments (usually with PayPal for a small fee). Then, once you've got the skin and bones of your website set up, it's time to start getting customers to make sales.

That's where digital marketing comes in. You'll need to drive traffic to your site. With marketing, there's no one-size-fits-all approach. You can opt for **organic growth strategies** by creating in-depth reviews of the products you're writing. Then, when people search for products like yours, they'll read your review and (hopefully) make the purchase. Or, another way of generating organic growth is creating quality content on topics related to your dropshipping products. For example, if you sell stainless steel water bottles, you can choose to write blog posts on the dangers of aluminum water bottles, or how stainless steel water bottles are reducing the amount of single-use plastics we consume, etc. Your goal is to create valuable and shareable content that then makes people stop and say, "Hey, maybe I should buy a stainless steel water bottle!"

You can also opt for paid marketing strategies, too. It may be scary to first time investors and freshly graduated college students with little to spend, but creating optimized **Pay Per Click ads** (PPC ads) can be a real game changer and lead to huge returns on your investment! This method is especially useful for dropshippers with trendy items (like fashion, accessories, or other items that have a short shelf-life in terms of perceived value). You can even run ads on your online dropshipping store or run promotions for products with Facebook, Instagram and Pinterest (which is often underutilized!).

But, before you even start creating the website and advertising it, there's one thing you need to do to minimize the risk of your dropshipping business failing: **research, research, research!** If you haven't spent time making sure you have a viable product with enough demand, you shouldn't even start creating your website! The very first step to creating a successful dropshipping business is ensuring you've found a successful niche. If you're the type of person who jumped straight into building Legos or Bionicles as a kid, this will be important for you to understand! While it's great to be creative and bend the rules at time, this is not the case here. It's best to approach dropshipping with a clear plan in mind, which means finding a profitable niche and feasible products to sell. In general, you want to find products that already have demand. If you choose to sell some exotic herbs like Incarvillea Sinensis, you'll have a much harder time than if you were to sell ginseng, for example, which the general population is more familiar with. But then, with ginseng, you run the risk of your product not being discovered since the market may be a bit too saturated. So, you'll have to come up with a product differentiation or pricing strategy to generate sales.

That's not all you have to think about when finding products. You also have to make sure your product can be shipped in a reasonable time (i.e. selling inflatable mattresses will incur more shipping expenses, thus cutting into your profit margins, than selling pillowcases, which are smaller and cheaper to sell). Then of course, you'll have to factor in the perceived value of your product. If you're selling a sheet of stickers priced at 10 cents on AliExpress, good luck selling them for more than a few dollars. But that fashionable emerald ring which costs $3, on the other hand, can be sold for $50 if you've created the right 'digital staging' (i.e. grouping the product with a nice outfit, an attractive model, etc.).

What's the catch? If dropshipping were so easy and profitable, everyone would be doing it. But, the reality is, in most cases, your profit margins aren't that high. Think about it: you have to buy the product from AliExpress (usually at full price), cover the costs of the ads you run and pay the subscription fee to Shopify or BigCommerce, pay taxes, and then you're left with some profit - only after you've marked up the price of the product on your eCommerce store. This option does work, and there are thousands of success stories, but it's not easy to create a dropshipping website. If you think you have what it takes, I encourage you to do a Google (or DuckDuckGo) search on dropshipping, watch some YouTube videos or explore the topic further on Pinterest.

Quick Summary of Dropshipping

1. Determine Niche. Find an area that has demonstrated demand but isn't oversaturated with suppliers (i.e. avoid high-competition products). Ensure there's sufficient demand and the product is profitable.

2. Select Products to Sell (usually from AliExpress.com). You'll want to determine the right balance between quality and price and ensure your product margins are significant enough to make a profit. Don't neglect the seller's rating and experience - you want to ensure the products are delivered on time.

3. Create an eCommerce Shop Online. If you have experience and time, you can select the WooCommerce route via WordPress (the good news: it's free! All you need is a domain name and web hosting). If you want something quick and easy, opt for Shopify, Wix, or BigCommerce (but keep in mind: you'll be paying more).

4. Market Your eCommerce Shop. Now that you've laid the foundation, have a functioning website and a smooth payment platform, it's time to get the word out. You can use social media like Facebook, Instagram and Pinterest. Each of those programs have their own pros and cons. You may even consider using paid marketing if you don't have a large following or page likes. Then, you may decide to use SEO tactics and inbound traffic strategies such as blog writing to get people onto your website and browsing your products. There are all kinds of strategies to market your dropshipping business. The important thing is that you explore your options, find a few strategies that work, and pursue them further each day.

5. Customer Satisfaction and Repeat Business. Once you make a sale, it doesn't end there. You need to ensure your sellers in China (or wherever they are in the world!) are delivering your products on time. Afterall - you don't want to damage your brand that you've worked so hard to build and market. After ensuring everything is clear on the supplier's end, you'll want to make sure buyers come back to your page. Are you using email marketing effectively on a regular basis? Running seasonal promotions? Creating a rewards program? These are the types of ideas you want to explore for repeat business.

Blogging

Blogging isn't just for travelers or personal diaries anymore. You can make serious money blogging. Blogging originally existed as a creative outlet for people to share their thoughts and photos, but now it's evolved into a serious money making machine for many. But, keep in mind: most people aren't raking in tons of dough with this option, in fact Lifehacker gathered the following information on the average salaries of bloggers:

"Salaries for bloggers vary widely. This report from Glassdoor shows ranges from $19K to $79K a year for the title "blogger," while other sources say the 14% of bloggers who earn a salary make, on average, $24K a year (or $33K for corporate bloggers). Likewise, freelance bloggers can make anything from under $10 a post to $100 or more for a relatively short post.

As for running your own blog, a survey of 1,000 bloggers by Blogging.com in 2012 found that 17% are able to sustain their lifestyle or support their family with their blogs, while 81% never make even $100 from blogging. The other 2% spend less than 2 hours a day blogging but make more than $150K (Tim Ferriss types).

Another survey, this one of 1,500 ProBlogger readers who said they're trying to make money by blogging, found that 9% make between $1,000 and $10,000 a month and 4% make over $10,000 a month. But the vast majority makes less than $3.50 per day. (Most of these were blogs less than two years old, though.)"

What does this mean? How much money can you expect to see? It depends. While income reports of bloggers vary, they seem to follow the 80/20 rule: 80% of bloggers make no to little money each month, while 20% are making money (at least $100 or more). The reason that most bloggers aren't making money is likely because most are "hobby" bloggers and aren't blogging for profit. Their goal isn't profit but rather to express themselves online. Or, contrarily, they simply haven't figured out how to monetize their blog effectively.

There are a variety of ways to monetize a blog. According to Brandong Gaille from the Blog Millionaire Podcast, of blogs making between $2,500 and $7,500 per month, the following monetization strategies are used:

- 35% of their money is made from **ads**
- 27% from **affiliates**
- 14% from **sponsored posts**
- 7% from **services/consulting**
- 3% from **online courses**

As you can see, there are a variety of ways for you to make money with blogging. A blog is simply a platform that exists to: A. Provide value to your reader base and those who stumble upon your blog. In other words: blogging is meant to provide resources and valuable content to readers; it's sole focus is not to make money like an eCommerce site or selling on eBay. It's much more complex than that and entails expressing value to your readers before you make any sales. And B. The purpose of your blog is also to make money. When your blog is monetized, you can sell products - either your own or from others (i.e. affiliate marketing) and also ad space and other premium content options.

Want to start blogging for profit? Here's how it's done. Again: this is a basic, non-detailed outline to give you an idea. Think of it more as a framework rather than an actual game-plan to follow. To start off, you want to pick a niche. As a blogger, you don't want to bite off more than you can chew. For example, you don't want to cover "supplements" as that's too vague and broad for a one-man (or one-woman) blogger. Instead, you want to break it down further: you can choose to focus your blog on adaptogenic herbal supplements, natural supplements to improve sleep quality, supplements to support the liver, etc. The point is to take a topic and break it down into something more tangible that you can do a good job covering.

And when you pick your niche, you must ensure it's something you're passionate about. While you can write about personal finance and different stock portfolios to invest in, it may be hard if you're not interested in finance. Your passions and interests should guide your decision in choosing your niche; not just money. Afterall, blogging is content-heavy (which means you'll be writing or making videos **a lot** so you want to make sure you already have some background knowledge and interest in the topic). Next, you also want to make sure the selected niche is profitable. This means you have to do some research in advance (as always!). Some questions to ask yourself before selecting a niche are:

- **How many people are searching for this topic on Google each month?** (Hint: use Google AdWords planner or "Ubersuggest" from neilpatel.com)

- **What types of affiliate programs are available?** (Hint: try looking on clickbank.com or other affiliate marketing program websites. These will come in hand down the road when you're ready to monetize your blog)
- **What are the demographics that this niche attracts?** (For example, if your niche is on budget travelers, expect to find a lot of young people who don't have tons of money to spend on your products. You would have to focus more on advertisement revenue or selling lots of low-cost products to your audience. Contrastingly, if you focus on upscale travel experience, you'll likely attract retirees and the 1% and can therefore sell less high-ticket items and make the same - or even more - than you would selling a large volume to a budget audience)

The Most Profitable Blogging Niches

This is a study from the Blog Income Report and the Blog Millionaire Podcast, which ranks blogging niches by their median monthly income:

- **Food** ($9,169)
- **Personal Finance** ($9,100)
- **Lifestyle** ($5,199)
- **Mommy** ($5,150)
- **Travel** ($5,000)
- **Marketing** ($4,269)

Note that the above niches aren't very "honed down". To increase your chance of success, you need to **narrow your niche down even further.** Let's take the first niche topic, as an example. Food is pretty generic, but we can focus on something more specific like Italian food. Then, making it even *more* specific, we can write about Italian pastries or Italian pasta. Don't like Italian food? That's fine! You can write about desserts! But not just any desserts. You can focus on cheese cake or cupcakes or even gluten-free cookies. Taking the next topic, Personal Finance, you'd also want to break that down into something unique to avoid competing for traffic in an already saturated market. If you notice there is a lack of resources for starting businesses for college students, you could focus your blog around that niche topic. Or, you can focus on financing strategies to own an affordable home by the age of 30. Or, on the flipside, you can focus on retiring internationally and helping your readers discover the most advantageous, cost-saving countries to retire in around the world.

The point is to choose something **specific**: dissect a topic into something that's not too much to chew off. Also, don't let the median income per niche influence your decision too much. For example, the Mommy-type blogs don't make as much money as other niches. Even if you choose to create a Mommy blog, keep in mind you can always incorporate higher-ticket affiliate strategies like marketing credit cards as an affiliate. If your main motivation in choosing your niche is profit, you're going to have a terribly hard time producing content about something you don't enjoy! So remember to be specific, write about a topic you're passionate about and realize that you can find creative strategies to monetize most niches if you have a sizable audience.

After choosing your niche and thorough research, you'll need to **create your website.** There are a bunch of different platforms to use, but most use WordPress and chances are you'll use wordpress, too. In fact, according to W3Techs, 35.7% of all content management systems users have chosen Wordpress. Additionally, they control 62.4% of the market. This means that WordPress is probably the best option for you. And a major perk: it's (almost) free. All you need to pay for is web hosting and your domain name.

To save money, you can learn to create your own website on your own with WordPress (if you've got some tech skills or grew up using MySpace, I highly recommend this option). If not, you can always pay someone to build the website for you. You can turn to a freelancing website like Fiverr or Upwork (which I don't recommend since you have to weed through several profiles to find quality service providers). Or, contact someone locally or online to build a website for you. If you have money to spend, investing in a professionally made website can save you a lot of time and hassle.

After your website is built and you have several important pages mapped out with content added to it (for example, a home page and about page) it's time to start **churning out content**. Yes - you're going to have to put in serious work. If your writing skills aren't strong or you just downright down like to write, blogging isn't for you. Keep in mind: you don't have to be the best writer either. There's no need to be a wordsmith like an author and no need to be formal as you would in academia. You do, however, have to produce high-quality content that is valuable for readers. That means when people search the web for 'best beach towns in Italy', for example, you don't just list off a bunch of random towns. Rather, you take the time to research each destination (or write from your travel experience), include high quality photos and other relevant information (like a packing list, insider tips, etc.). That way, the content is likely to be shared by your readers on social media and ranked higher on Google. All of which are important strategies for increasing your inbound traffic.

You've got some blog posts up but aren't seeing any results. Now what? Next, you need to focus on **gaining regular readers** and **marketing** your content. You can gain regular readers by creating quality content on a regular basis (again: I keep emphasising quality because it's so important. Each piece you write needs to provide value of some sort. Go into detail, provide specific examples, use images and maps and other visual cues) and take advantage of an email list. If you want to start attracting new readers (outside of your friends and family. That's an important first step: share your content first with people who are likely to support you. Don't be shy; there are more people rooting for you than you think!) you're going to need to develop a marketing plan. This is especially key for new blogs. New blogs don't get much organic traffic growth right off the bat from search engines. In other words, Google won't "crawl" your website and posts for a few weeks. Crawling simply means indexing your website on the search engine via a mysterious algorithm. So, that means you're going to need to use some form of social media.

What are the best ways to **market your blog posts with social media?** As mentioned, start marketing your content to people who are already on your team. They're going to help you by clicking on your blog posts and sharing it with their friends, on Facebook and Instagram, etc. thus creating a "snowball effect". Next, you want to create social media accounts for your blog. Facebook and Instagram are the most widely used, but you can't neglect Pinterest! Don't just use your personal account to market your products. You want to think long term and use your blog's name when you create your social media accounts. You then need to gather followers, which is another topic in and of itself. To give you a quick summary, you do this by compiling and sharing valuable content (for example, if you're selling dog toys, you'd want to share blog posts on your social media page on how to train a dog, the best dog breeds for families, etc.) It's important to keep things light and non-spammy. Nobody wants to log onto Facebook and Instagram to be advertised to. As a general rule of thumb, advertise your own blog and products/affiliates once every ten posts. It's crucial to interact with others, too. Be sure to comment on others' posts, like other pages and initiate a conversation with other people. Be genuine in your comments and interactions, and again: don't be spammy!

Using the dog toy example again, you wouldn't want to comment on a competitor's page and say something like 'great post! If you want even better dog toys, visit www.xyz.com'. Also, you don't want to leave comments on others' posts that provide no value or are generic while shamelessly promoting your own website. For example: 'great post! Visit www.xyz.com'. That comment is unhelpful and adds nothing to the discussion. It's simply a cheap way for you to get clicks back to your website (and most people won't click - it's just a waste of time). Instead, skim through an article and find something you like about it. For example, if someone shares a post on Facebook about why Golden Retrievers are great dogs, use your Facebook page to comment something like: "I agree! I've had my Golden for 3 years now and she's part of the family now." This way, you've left the link to your website off (which shows that you're genuinely interested). Other people will see that you've commented - and if they're curious - they'll then click on your Facebook page. Once they're on your Facebook page and see you've (hopefully) been producing and sharing valuable content, they'll then visit your website. And that's how social media marketing works on all platforms, essentially. It's a delicate balance between sharing your own content and products; sharing high-quality content from others; and interacting with other social media users by liking and commenting. After a while, you should accumulate new page likes and followers.

Now, let's look at the hypothetical situation you'd be in after a few months of creating content and marketing it on social media: you now have several posts (if you can publish posts weekly or more - even better), your likes and follows have increased, and your website's traffic is starting to pick up (especially because Google has started to index your website and a few of your posts were shared often). Now what? It's time to **monetize**! You've put in the hard work and created valuable content...why not get paid for it? You should look on sites like Clickbank.com or contact businesses directly. Many times, you can type in "<your niche> + affiliates" and discover brands and companies to work with. Once you've been approved for their affiliate programs, the options of incorporating their products into your website are endless! You can write an entire post on their product, review their product, or simply link to it in one of your blog posts where appropriate. For example, if you're creating a website to teach others how to make money online, you can create a link to a web hosting business with an affiliate program. If people buy or click, you would then be credited with a commission.

Other ways to monetize your blog are with **Google ads** and **sponsored posts**. With Google ads, you can place ads relevant to your niche within your website. Each time someone clicks on the link, you get a small commission. As you saw in the statistics above regarding sources of revenue for bloggers, this is the biggest source of earnings for bloggers making over $2,000. Keep in mind, you can also sell ad space privately to a business or use another means of connecting with advertisers besides Google Ads. As for sponsored posts, a company pays you to feature their product in one of your posts. You may be paid a one lump sum, or you could get paid depending upon the number of views the post gets. That's for you to decide when you reach an agreement with businesses that want a sponsored post on your website. But, keep in mind, this usually only happens after you're getting significant traffic to your website (we're talking at least 10,000 visits per month).

One important thing to note: **don't be a sell-out** to your audience. And in general, it's just not ethical to promote bad products in order to make a quick buck. Be sure to only market products that you trust, believe in and that actually work. As you're scrolling through Clickbank or any other affiliate network and see a product with a 70% commision, don't incorporate it in your blog just for the money. It's important to think long-term, which is why you need to provide your readers with products that are actually effective and are fairly priced.

Now that you've created a website with a sizable following and regular traffic (which, in general takes at least six months. There are no get rich quick schemes!) it's important that you continue to engage people who follow your blog. Not everyone is going to be interested in keeping up with every single one of your posts, but many will. Those people who gobble up your content will also be the ones who you sell to most. Many others are just passing through, having stumbled upon your website from Google or having clicked on your post from Facebook (and that's OK - you can still make sales with them. But for many bloggers, most of their sales come from their regular readers!). Since your regulars are so important, you want to continue to engage with them. One of the best ways to do this is with **email**. Create a weekly, bi-weekly or monthly newsletter and continue to provide them value. That way, they keep coming back to your blog. One of the best ways of getting an email from your readers is providing something **free** that's valuable. It can be an inexpensive product that you mail to them, a workbook, a PDF, a premium video, or even an ebook. Also, you can consider using a notification system for those you want to keep up with all your posts. And there you have it: these are a few ways to keep your readers engaged, coming back for more!

As you can understand, creating a blog takes a lot of patience, trial and error, and time! It's not a get rich quick scheme, and in fact, most will give up trying to make money from their blog. Overall, blogging is a great tool to supplement your income - and, you may even be able to quit your job and pursue blogging full time! If you think you have what it takes and love writing, start your blogging journey now (remember to pick a niche and do your due diligence first, though!).

Quick Summary of Blogging

1. Define Your Niche. Your niche should be something you're passionate about or have lots of knowledge in. Brainstorm a list of topics you're interested in, and then narrow it down: of all the topics, which can you write about the most? What's the topic you can't stop talking about to your friends? Once you've identified that, you can start researching.

2. Research, Research, Research. It's not enough to just be passionate and knowledgeable about a certain subject. You may be passionate about snails, for example. How can you monetize snails? Since they're not an ideal pet and aren't often seen as a tasty snack, there's no money to be made blogging about snails (or is there? Maybe

I'm wrong!). But, is there money to be made blogging about luxury watches, fancy red wines or camping? Sure. Just make sure there's not too much competition and you have enough ideas to create regular, quality content.

3. Build Your Website. Either hire someone to create a website for you or learn how to do it on your own with WordPress. You want to make sure your website is user-friendly, clean and matches the tone of your content and topic.

4. Create Valuable Content. Here comes the laborious part: you have to write. Make it a point to write something most days of the week. I highly recommend creating a writing schedule or setting a minimum word count goal each day so that you can regularly produce content. It's also invaluable to learn the basics of SEO (search engine optimization) to ensure your content is getting picked up by Google.

5. Market Your Content. Be resourceful, and at times, think outside of the box. Always remember you have your "cheerleaders" (i.e. friends and family) who will support you no matter what. After asking your friends and family to help spread the word and share your posts, it's time to expand and do some social media marketing. If you're just starting out and don't have a huge budget, I recommend straying away from paid advertising.

6. Choose Monetization Methods. You can choose to sprinkle affiliate marketing links in your post, incorporate google ad banners on your website, connect with brands to create sponsored content or even sell your own products. The world of monetizing your blog is your oyster. Just remember to preach quality and don't go after cheap sales. A good rule of thumb is: if you wouldn't use a product yourself, chances are you shouldn't market it on your blog to others.

7. Keep Growing Your Email List and Traffic. If you're producing quality content on a regular basis, your traffic is going to increase. It's important that you start collecting emails so that you can continue to provide valuable content - and affiliate products - to your readers. Your goal is to turn one-time browsers into lifelong readers.

Influencer Marketing

We have already touched on utilizing affiliate marketing strategies above in blogging, but being an "influencer" is a bit different. While blogging is niche-centered, being an influencer is more person-centered. In other words: the influencer is the star of their own brands. To further clarify, blogging is about creating content (monstely written) that attracts visitors to a blog. Bloggers then get money when they make digital sales, get clicks on affiliate links, or display ads, etc. Influencer marketing, on the other hand, is about working with a brand(s) or business(es) and employing a variety of marketing techniques to help sell the product from a variety of platforms - not just a blog.

Let me give you an example to help break it down. If you're an Instagram model or "influencer" that has several thousands of followers, you can then work with brands to promote their products using your Instagram posts. This can be done by sharing their product in your story, creating a post featuring their product, or by mentioning the business in your caption. You would be paid beforehand depending upon the predetermined agreement you've negotiated with the business requiring your service. This is often seen with tea products, where companies enlist attractive models to pose with their slimming teas (and often falsely claim that their physiques are the result of the tea) in order to make more sales. But, affiliate marketing isn't always that shady. There are plenty of products and businesses out there that have reputable products that want to leverage the traffic and following of other people to spread the word about their product.

That's the essence of influencer marketing: taking advantage of your existing sources of traffic and directing them to a product or service in exchange for payment. You may get paid a one lump sum, be paid per click (PPC), or you may only be paid when one of your followers makes a purchase. Again, this is different from blogging since blogging involves creating valuable content to make money in a variety of methods while affiliate marketers generally work with a few products using their sources of traffic or followers as a way to make sales.

If you're wondering how to get into influencer marketing, the answer is: you need to start building up your followers. As always, before you even begin digging in and creating content, you need to determine a niche first. For example, if you have a computer science degree and nerd out on hardware and software, you can decide to create a YouTube channel reviewing different laptops or software programs. Or, if you've got a cute face and a swimsuit-ready body, you may consider putting it to use on Instagram where some influencers make millions of dollars each year. Choosing your niche is a bit more trial and error than blogging. You may decide to become a travel photographer and plan on taking pictures of landscapes all over the world, only to notice that pictures of white sand beaches get you double the likes than pictures of the desert. While this virtual business structure is called "Influencer Marketing", ironically, content producers who are making the most profit are influenced by their followers tastes and preferences, and not the other way around. In other words: you'll have to produce content that your followers like - and that may not be what you like, **personally**.

Choosing the Right Platform

After coming up with a loose idea on what you can post about, it's time to bring the idea to life. You'll have to decide on a social media channel to make your big debut:

Blogging

As previously mentioned, you can become an "influencer" by creating valuable content in your field. The more content you produce, the more likely you'll become an authority figure and thus, the more likely businesses will want to work with you to promote their products or services.

YouTube

Like producing short movies? Want to start a mini series online? Do you enjoy talking in front of a camera? If so, YouTube may be best! Not only can you become an influencer on YouTube and make money via affiliate marketing, you can also use YouTube's ads feature (as long as your content falls within their community guidelines, which can be strict. Many YouTube content producers have been demonetized). You can start a makeup tutorial channel, for example. Once you gain a significant following, beauty companies may pay you to use their product and feature it in a video. Or, maybe you're creating a political channel, covering current events. You may have companies that want to sponsor your videos if you talk about them for thirty seconds before you start your spiel. In essence, that's how YouTube works - you show off products and advertise businesses to your subscribers and viewers.

Facebook

Facebook is a bit different. The typical Facebook user is changing as many of its younger users have migrated to Instagram. However, you can still leverage your Facebook, nonetheless. With Facebook, you can use videos, write posts, or add pictures to gain followers. If you have the right amount of followers and cover an important niche, you may start accepting offers from businesses looking to advertise their products to your following.

Instagram

Instagram is probably the most well-known form of influencer marketing. Since Instagram is very visual in nature, many beauty, fashion, lifestyle and health businesses choose to use affiliates on Instagram. If you want to go the instagram route, be sure to post on a consistent schedule and realize there are four main types of Instagrammers: casual users (those who aren't trying to monetize their Instagram and usually just post at randow with no strategy), informational accounts (which post things like quotes, infographics and facts and figures), photography accounts (most of these types of accounts focus on a specific theme: wild animals, Africa, castles, cars, etc. The quality of the photos is much higher than casual users), and people accounts (this category is ruled by selfie kings and queens, models, fitness models, and also people who create funny short skits and videos). Instagram can be a great way to create engaging content, and it usually takes less work than blogging. However, blogging is a more secure form of earning money, unlike Instagram (i.e. after six months, you're bound to get significant traffic if you're posting quality articles, using SEO and sharing on social media, whereas with Instagram not everyone becomes 'instafamous').

Goodreads

This sounds crazy, but if you've got a lot of followers on your Goodreads account, you can take advantage of that fact and let authors come to you. Many are willing to pay you to leave a review, write a post on their book, or simply mark that you're reading their book.

Podcasts

Don't want to show your face on camera? Are you better with your words than you are in front of the camera (or behind it)? If so, podcasting may be right for you! The good thing about podcasts is that not many people are doing it compared to other platforms. That means you have a higher chance of being discovered. When you create a podcast, you can run it on a podcast broadcasting platform (with Apple, on Spotify, etc.) post it on Facebook and Instagram, and even post the recording on YouTube with a slideshow presentation or simple image. If you have a smartphone, you can start right now! After gaining a few listeners, you may decide to invest in a quality microphone for a better listening experience for your audience. Podcasts work just like the radio as far as monetization. You can reach an agreement with businesses to talk about their product or services on your show, or conversely, you can let them produce an ad and plug it into your show.

In Person

Don't forget about the good ol' fashion way of making sales in person. If you're sociable and don't mind small talk with strangers, this is the perfect way to become an "influencer marketer". This can be done by selling software with a unique discount code that corresponds to your profile, for example. If and when the person you're talking to decides to purchase the software using your discount code, you'll get a commision deposited into your bank account. Or, you can create a website and give people you meet a business card with a link to your website. Once they browse your website and click on your sales page for travel deals, for example, and make a purchase, you'll be credited. You can also become a "brand representative" and sell products from a brochure to people (think Mary Kay, Avon, Herbalife, etc.) The downside, however, is that most people see through these selling multi-level marketing schemes and realize the products are fairly low quality or generic and overpriced.

You can find smaller companies to sell with that focus on quality, however. If you decide to travel, you can make sales on the go, internationally, too!

There are other channels and ways to gather a following for you to discover! One thing to realize: sometimes it's not about the quantity of your followers but rather the trust you've established with them and their propensity to buy. For example, somebody on YouTube with only 10,000 subscribers that reviews iPhones and apps can make more money than a fitness model with a hundred thousand subscribers. The iPhone and app reviewer will usually be pitching higher value items to interested buyers while the fitness model may sell online coaching, meal plans, exercise plans, tea, etc. which aren't priced as high. And also, if the fitness model is making exercise videos, chances are people are coming there for free content and aren't as likely to buy. The point is, you want to accumulate followers, but as always: quality reigns over quantity.

Social Media Automation

After selecting the right platform for building your audience, you need to start posting regularly. If on Instagram and Facebook, that means posting daily. If on YouTube, that usually means posting once or twice a week. To avoid disappointing your audience, you need to post on a regular basis to ensure your current followers are satisfied and reach more followers. Make a schedule and stick to it. It may seem like a lot of work, but there are several apps and software programs that can help you schedule and automate the process.

Tailwind
Tailwind allows you to join tribes (i.e. other content producers who you interact with and pin their content in exchange for pins on your posts,

too) to help boost your Instagram presence. Additionally, you can schedule pins automatically, saving you lots of time.

Later
Later.com allows you to schedule posts for Facebook, Instagram, Pinterest and Twitter. It's the top scheduler for Instagram and many use it to conveniently place links in their bio on Insta. It can help save your precious time, allowing you to create posts effortlessly and quickly.

Facebook's Post Scheduler
Instead of using a third-party program, you can use Facebook directly to program posts. Whether paid or free, you can schedule posts easily on Facebook. All you need is a business account onFacebook to get started.

Buffer
Buffer is an excellent social media automation platform to use for all the major social media platforms. While Buffer used to be free, they now only offer paid subscriptions starting at $15 per month. Buffer can be useful in the future when you're making more in profit as an influencer and can cover the costs.

Hootsuite
Hootsuite is another social media automation platform like Buffer and Later. For $25 per month (a bit more expensive than Buffer), you can schedule your posts as an influencer from 10 social media accounts. Hootsuite is one of the best, and original, social media scheduling platforms.

Once you've found your posting rhythm and a schedule that works for you, it's time to do a bit of **A/B testing**. What does that mean? Basically, you need to measure what's getting you the most response.

One week, you may post pictures on Instagram of sunny beaches, the next you may take pictures in the jungle. Compare the two results: which one got the most likes? The most views? Which one led to the most affiliate sales? Those are the questions you need to ask yourself and should guide the content you create. While you may *personally* enjoy snapping pictures of the beach, if your audience responds to the jungle more, that's probably the area you should focus on - that is, if you want to be a strategic influencer marketer and maximize your monetization strategy. You can also test things like using emojis or keeping the text plain, writing full paragraphs or sticking to just a few lines, using dozens of hashtags or sticking to just a few. Each time you post something, change a variable and see if that responds better than your previous posts. To deliver the best content, you need to become a scientist.

Another thing to keep in mind: social media moves fast! Just as you've planned out an entire week of content on Turin, Italy, wildfires could break out, earthquakes could happen, major political events can shake the world (though, it's a bit risky to get too political). That could cause you to make a quick post to express your sympathy for people experiencing massive wildfires in another corner of the world, for example. There are also lots of trends on Instagram, Facebook and Youtube (e.g. the Ice Bucket Challenge, 10 Year Challenge, etc.) If you're a 'people account' capitalizing on these trends are especially important. While they may seem silly, they can be a great way for you to gain exposure.

After growing your audience and focusing on creating quality posts, chances are there will be a few brands that want to work with you. That means money in your pocket! Again, as with monetizing your blog and using affiliates, you don't want to choose crummy products. You want to stick to promoting products or services that you would use yourself. If you try to sell a 'fidget spinner', for example, at $30 a piece, those who bought it will likely feel ripped off and unfollow you. And even those who haven't bought into something may get tired of you trying to push terrible products down their throat. So, be careful with the products you use - it can really affect your business in the long run. Also, you don't want to be too pushy. There's nothing worse than someone constantly trying to sell a product with every post. You may find you make more sales when you promote a product every other post, or every four posts, etc. Find something that works for you and try to make sales without being 'salesy'.

Quick Summary of Affiliate Marketing

1. Choose a Niche. As always, you want to pick something that you specifically rock in. What are you naturally talented in? What's your expertise? What are you passionate about? Pursue those areas further. But first - make sure there's a market for it (i.e. there are related products you can pitch to an audience and businesses are willing to pay).

2. Pick a Channel for Creating Content. If you're best at photography, pick Instagram since it's very visual. Do you write witty captions and like a blend of all content types (videos, memes, photos, etc.)? Then, perhaps Facebook is best. Like making videos and have a nice camera you want to put to use? Go with YouTube (Bonus: YouTube is a search engine. That means unlike Instagram and Facebook which are very time-dependent platforms, your content can appear long after you've posted the video!).

3. Post Regularly. You don't want to flood someone's feed one day with multiple posts then go missing for weeks right after. Make your content in advance and utilize a scheduling app to be sure you're always on track and on time with your posts. Some influencers are able to knock out all of their posts weeks - or even a month - in advance.

4. Stay On Top of Trends and Continue to Create What Gets the Best Response. Be prepared for curveballs. The modern world changes so quickly. Trends come and go. As an influencer, people expect you to stay on top of trends more than the typical social media user. Keep that in mind as you develop a social media strategy. Also, if something's not working for you - change it. If you're getting regular growth using a similar type of photo or video - keep it. Your audience should determine the kind of content you produce. Read comments and check your feedback.

5. Find Businesses to Work With. Here comes the fun part: putting your posts and videos to work for you. Sometimes business will contact you directly for a paid partnership, other times you'll need to seek them out. Remember that making a few quick bucks isn't the goal (i.e. focus on a long-term growth strategy and only choose quality products).

6. Don't Oversell. Your audience likely started following you because you posted funny videos, because you're nice to look at, or because you post interesting guides and content. Don't ruin your image by constantly pushing products on your audience. Instead, pick maybe one or two products to focus on each post (i.e. not all of the products you work with) and weave it into your content. Don't splatter the sale - make sure it fits the theme of your post and provides value. Remember, your audience started following you for a reason - try to be authentic to that.

Selling a Physical Product Online

Who says you have to open a shop and be tied to a physical location to sell products? While opening a brick and mortar business can be profitable, the downside is it comes with more expenses (i.e. paying rent or buying a space for your shop and requiring personnel to work there, etc.) That's where selling a product (or multiple products!) online comes in. Instead of facing tons of startup costs, you can focus on creating great products (or sourcing them) and creating a website that generates you tons of sales.

But first: how is this different than dropshipping? The main difference lies in the fact that you're responsible for the product and storing the product. Even if you're traveling the world, you will need to hire someone or trust a family member to store and ship your product. There are other means of automating this process (for example, implementing 'Fulfilment by Amazon' or FBA, which handles storing and shipping your product) which can make running your business more hands-off. This usually results in lowered profit, however. But on the upside, at least you have more freedom and flexibility. If you're sold on the idea of creating your own products and selling them online - great! But before we get ahead of ourselves, there's something you need to do before you even start thinking about a formula or design for your product. As always: research, research, research.

You may think that you've come up with an amazing product - but the real question is: do other people think so, too? For example, let's say you've invented an electric boomerang that you think is going to revolutionize the world! The (hypothetical) problem? Frisbees are much more popular than boomerangs. Instead of trying to "reinvent the wheel" by educating and advertising how cool your boomerang product is, it may be best to opt for something similar but more popular: in this case, the frisbee. Now that you've established there's a demand for frisbees, you realize there's yet another problem: there's a little too much demand. The market is saturated. Plus, you have a lot of big toy manufacturing companies that are able to keep their costs down due to the "economies of scale" effect by buying wholesale, so they dominate the market and can make way more sales at a lower price. You've hit a deadend. Or have you? Maybe you need to focus on product differentiation. Instead of making a plastic frisbee like your competition, you may decide to make a frisbee out of bamboo - at a higher cost for consumers. But, consumers may be willing to pay: it's much cooler than a plastic frisbee, plus it's better for the environment and captures the attention of people trying to live greener.

In summary: choosing the right product is a delicate balance between innovation and meeting existing consumer demands. If you create a product that's too innovative (in the example above, the electric boomerang) you risk spending too much on marketing your product and educating consumers. On the flipside, if you create a product with tons of existing consumer demand (in this case, a plain ol' frisbee), you risk not being able to penetrate the market. In order to differentiate your product, you opt to add an innovative twist on an existing product: a bamboo frisbee.

After ensuring you have a feasible product that's neither too innovative nor oversaturated with competitors, you have to create the product itself. Will you create it yourself at home or in the kitchen? Or, will you have engineers create it for you? Will it be produced domestically in your country? Or, will you outsource your product to China, India or Bangladesh where the cost of labor is cheaper (and the quality of your product will likely be lower)? These are the issues you need to think about when contemplating creating a product.

To give you an idea of how the product creation process is, I once tried to make a product to sell: lip balm (though, it wasn't successful to be honest! I didn't even try marketing the product since I was so busy. But hear me out: I did create a nice product). While the product didn't take off and I didn't create a website for it or sell on Etsy, at a farmer's market, in person, etc. it still serves as a guide for determining the right ingredients for a product.

Here's how strategic product creation looks. Even if you're making something completely different, it's important to understand the thought-process behind creating a product and selecting the right materials:

Plastic lip balm tubes (I ordered 250 from China with Alibaba). At the time, I opted for plastic tubes since they were cheap and this is how most consumers expect to find lip balm. If I wanted to do something more eco-friendly, I could have opted for glass jars or a recycled material and increased the price of the product to cover the expense.

Unrefined white beeswax. I wanted the product to be natural and therefore I opted for an unrefined beeswax. This helps keep the product together - without the beeswax, there would be nothing to solidify the oils which wouldn't be fun on a warm day.

Organic coconut oil. I chose organic coconut oil since it's high in saturated fats and has a high smoke point. Thus, it's solid at room temperature and makes the product more stable and less likely to become runny when the temperature is warm. Also note I opted for organic coconut oil. Not canola oil, industrial seed oils or vegetable oil (which are extremely heat sensitive and create free radicals in the body). While many consumers aren't aware of the inflammatory effects of certain pesticides and genetically modified organisms (GMO's) I wanted to cater to a health-conscious market that's looking for a high-quality, non toxic, organic product. Afterall - it's going on the lips!

Extra virgin olive oil from Italy. To balance out the coconut oil I added olive oil. Coconut oil is more moisturizing since it's so rich in saturated fats, while extra virgin olive oil is more readily absorbed by the skin.

Essential oils. To give the lip balm some flavor and a nice fragrance, I used a blend of essential oils. I didn't use synthetic fragrance oils since, again, I was catering to a natural crowd that's looking for a higher quality product.

Printed labels. Instead of spending more money on individually printed labels that may be a better quality, I took a regular sized sheet of paper and fit as many small labels on there as I could fit. I printed it out on adhesive paper without any finish on it (which was a mistake - the printed paper easily rubbed off when wet) and cut out several dozens of labels per sheet by hand with scissors.

And *voila*! A potentially successful product was born. You want to address product costs, buying from China when necessary to save money, or using domestically produced ingredients for a higher quality product. Also, you need to keep in mind how your product is going to last from start to finish (for example, printing on regular adhesive paper was a mistake since it rubbed off so easily). When you're researching and selecting a product, there's a tradeoff between innovation and market saturation. Product creation involves a tradeoff between **cutting costs** (e.g. using plastic tubes from China and regular paper labels) and **delivering value** (e.g. using only natural low-to-no toxic materials).

Another strategy that's less hands-on is buying and reselling a product. You can buy a bunch of pens with a frog design on them, for example, and sell them on eBay, Amazon or your very own eCommerce shop. Heck - you can even create an entire eShop or brand on frog-related merchandise: from backpacks to notebooks to watches and more. The key is, very obviously, to buy the products at a lower cost than you sell them. That means all the money you spend on advertising the product, shipping the product, storing the product and purchasing the product must be above the price you sell the product.

One thing you may have noticed with selling a physical product online: it requires a **larger financial investment.** If you aren't willing to spend $50 to a few thousand on developing a product or acquire an inventory then don't bother with this method. If you do have a bit of money to spend and are willing to take a risk - go for it!

As with dropshipping and blogging, you'll need a website or an eCommerce platform to sell your products. As previously mentioned, you can create your own website and use Wordpress and WooCommerce, or you can go for a more turnkey option like Shopify, BigCommerce or Wix. But that's not all; you can also sell your products on eCommerce platforms. Some sellers decide to sell exclusively on these platforms, others decide to sell on their own website (since ePlatforms often charge fees and take a percentage of your sales), while others use both strategies (which is recommended for maximum profit). Which eCommerce platform should you use? That all depends on your goals and type of product. In general, the most popular and powerful ones are Amazon (no surprise there!), eBay (especially for used and vintage goods), and Etsy (for handmade products).

Once you've mapped out which eCommerce platforms you want to sell with and have ideally created your own website, it's time to get into the nitty gritty of marketing. As I covered previously, it's important to take advantage of social media by sharing your products on Facebook, Instagram, Pinterest, Twitter, etc. Additionally, to drive traffic you need to make sure your website is optimized for search engines (SEO) by having enough content, the right keywords, powerful headlines, meta descriptions, alt tags for images and other SEO factors (SEO is such a huge topic - you'll have to research it on your own further. Or, if SEO is something you don't have the time or will to try for yourself, you can hire me at **RyanScottSEO.com**. I have monthly subscription plans that fit any budget).

Following successful marketing strategies like social media campaigns, email marketing, content marketing and keyword research (plus your own digital marketing methods. This is far from an exhaustive list. Do your own research and be creative. The sky's the limit with your marketing efforts!) you should have generated a few sales each month. In order to gain those coveted five-star reviews (which serve two purposes: 1. Positive ratings show you're doing a good job and your current customers are satisfied. It means the ratio of quality to price is OK and your delivery system is running smoothly. And 2. It's social proof. Potential buyers are more likely to buy products from sellers who have positive ratings. Speaking of ratings: since they're so important I'd greatly appreciate it if you could leave me a review - even if it's something short and sweet!), there are a few things you need to do. You need to ensure the quality of your product matches the price point, that you're delivering on time, and that you're not overselling your product in terms of its description. In other words: set realistic expectations for your buyers. If you claim your product is going to completely change your customers' lives or other claims - it better. If not, you're asking for 1-star reviews. That's why when you write your product descriptions, you want to pick your words very carefully. If you're selling a milk thistle supplement, for example, you don't want to claim that it will completely clean out your liver and cure cancer (which are both exaggerations and haven't been proven). Instead, you want to point to proven studies that demonstrate it has the capacity to help with liver detoxification and, as a result, may help decrease one's odds of cancer since the accumulation of toxicants in the body is known to contribute to cancer. See the difference? Pick your words carefully and avoid overpromising.

On another note, besides meeting realistic consumer expectations and delivering on time every time, there are strategies to encourage positive feedback and repeat business. For example, you can add a handwritten note with their purchase with a simple "Thanks for supporting a small business - see our website for other exciting products at www.ABC.com" or even add in a free, small sample of another product you offer. Adding a sample is a win-win: it adds even more value to the order and also gets the buyer to try another one of your products, thus increasing the probability they go back on your website or eCommerce profile and buy from you again. Additionally, you should always try to collect their email and send them a newsletter on a regular basis. This can be a great way to communicate expertise in your field and value, as well as market your products further. Another thing to do is ask for the review! Sometimes people need to be reminded or pushed in the right direction. As the adage goes: ask and you shall receive.

Quick Summary of Selling Physical Products Online

1. Research, Research, Research. You don't want to fully invest in a product until you know if there's a market and room for you in that market. Don't get carried away and start creating the product without doing proper research first - it could end up costing you hundreds or even thousands of dollars!

2. Develop (or Source) a Great Product. After determining there's a market for your potential product, it's time to take it from blueprint to a real, tangible product. You're either going to be experimenting with the formula or creation yourself. Or, you may have someone else manufacture it for you. Another successful strategy to keep in mind is buying from wholesalers and selling at a higher price than what you purchased plus expenses. Wholesalers don't have the time or capacity to sell at the consumer level. Their job is producing or distributing. That's where you come in with your sales-generating website and/or eCommerce platform and start making a profit!

3. Create a Captivating Website or Use a Selling Platform. Selling in the digital world almost always requires a website. Create a website on your own or pay someone to do it for you. Remember there are easy to use platforms like Wix, Shopify and BigCommerce, but the tradeoff is they come with high monthly expenses. If you have the time and skill, creating your own website can save you hundreds of dollars. Then, of course, you have the major selling platforms like Amazon, eBay and Etsy. If it's in your interest, make sure to take advantage of these platforms, too.

4. Market Your Shop. Once you've got an attractive website up and running, and/or a profile with your products uploaded to Amazon and other online selling platforms, it's time to start attracting your audience! While you may have a great product that generates its own traffic, you need to put in some work first. Get the word out about your product using SEO best practices, email marketing, social media and other marketing strategies.

5. Ensure Proper Delivery. You're not done after you make the sale! That's only half the battle. Since reviews and reputation are so important, you want to ensure you follow-up properly with your clients. This means fast delivery that's always on time. You may even want to provide extra goodies or personalization techniques to get buyers to come back for more. If you can, try to get your customer's email to continue to market to them and provide value and also ask for a review.

Selling e-Products

While this is similar to selling physical products (in fact, I was considering lumping them together into the same section) I wanted to point out an important distinction between selling physical products online and selling e-Products: Physical products require a **financial investment** while e-products require an investment far more valuable: **your time.** You can't just throw something invaluable together and call it an ecourse or ebook. You need to put in real sweat equity into what you do. While creating a physical product also takes time, and developing an e-product may take money, in general you're going to put way more effort into creating an e-course than you are a product. Additionally, e-products require little to no upfront money.

Take this ebook for example. This ebook was originally my thesis to graduate from my Business and Management program in Italy. It was supposed to be 15 to 20 pages anyway, so I told myself: why not spend a little more effort and time and create something that could (potentially) pay off forever? Why not create a little ebook and sell it on Amazon and my own website? And so, killing two birds with one stone, that's exactly what I did.

But, what did I have to sacrifice to create this article? My time of course. I was working 45 hours per week for my required internship and instead of tuning out and watching Netflix after working long hours, I forced myself to write *something* for this eBook. I also spent several hours skimming other blog posts, research reports and acquiring data to plug in to this book. This meant spending some of my Saturdays and Sundays hunched over my desk writing instead of hanging out with friends or being a couch potato. Will my efforts pay off? Hopefully. But even if they don't and I don't make crazy profit (which I'm not expecting to become a millionaire from this quick eBook anyway), at least I have something to show potential clients who would like to use my marketing or copywriting services.

That's something to keep in mind before you begin creating your digital product: there's no guarantee it'll be a success. There's a chance that all your time and efforts can lead to no financial gain. But, there's also a chance that you'll be successful, too. The key to increasing the chance of success is researching! For example, with this eBook I didn't blindly choose it because I'm passionate about creating a living online and traveling the world. Instead, I realized there were several articles being published about how the workforce is shifting from a traditional in-person one to one that is remote. I read an article entitled 'Why working from home should be standard practice' from Ideas.Ted.com that talked about the benefits of allowing employees to work at home. The article reported that a company, Ctrip, found that they, "'saved $1,900 per employee over the course of the study on office space…But to [their] amazement, the work-from-home employees were far from goofing off — they increased productivity by 13.5 percent over those working in the office. That's like getting an extra day's work from each employee.' The people working from home also reported shorter breaks and fewer sick days and took less time off." After reading this, and other sources, I knew that the modern workforce was changing and that there's potential demand for an ebook like this.

Also, I looked on Amazon Kindle and noticed there were other books out there, but none that gave realistic, concrete strategies to making money online while traveling and living cheaply abroad. And so, my eBook was born! I did my proper research and realized there's a market for the content I created. In summary, before you start investing your time into your digital project, you need to find there's a market first.

After determining there's sufficient demand for your eProduct, you then need to put in the work to create it. In case you're at a loss for what types of digital products you can sell, here are some ideas for inspiration:

eBooks
If you're willing to research or write about something you're passionate about, you can write an ebook relatively quickly (we're talking days to weeks). Or, if you're creative and want to tell a story, try fiction out.

eCourses
eCourses have a huge profit potential. In fact, some report more than ten times the profit with eCourses than they had writing eBooks (while spending a fraction of the time developing an eCourse since it mainly involves speaking in front of a camera).

Create and Flip Websites
Are you an expert at creating attractive website designs? Or creating content? You can develop websites and sell them at various stages. From freshly created, to fully-mature websites with tons of traffic. Try using a website like Flippa.com.

Sell Domain Names
There are people who make millions with those (though it remains a bit of a mystery to me!). All you need to do, in essence, is find domain

names that you think are going to become in-demand in the future. It's basically like buying digital real estate in the ghetto before hipsters come in and make it nice! You buy a domain name before it's in-demand by companies and sell it for a higher price.

Create Premium Templates for WordPress
If you're talented with WordPress and design, you have an opportunity to make passive income by selling premium themes. Sometimes standard, free themes just don't cut it on WordPress. Users may be looking for something more robust, which is where you meet that demand.

Make a Documentary or Movie and Sell It
If you're passionate about creating films, you can try your hand at creating your own film. Whether it's a short film or an entire series, you can sell it from your own website as a passive form of income. Or, you can accept donations on platforms like Patreon for your premium content.

Diet or Exercise Plans
This is a popular option for fitness influencers on Instagram and YouTube. People see nice bodies and people in the gym and want to get a beach body, too. If you have a nice body or are a nutritionist, consider creating a generic diet regimen you can sell en masse. Or, you can create customized plans (which is a bit more hands-on, but can earn you more money).

Premium Content
If you have a popular blog and want to profit on your high traffic or have a bunch of dedicated readers, you can offer content - at an expense. Whether you go more in-depth on a free post you've written on, or cover special topics, that's for you to decide. If your content is

quality and you have regular readers, chances are some are willing to pay or more.

Coaching

If you're good at something - from crafting to parenting, diet and exercise, and more, you can capitalize on your knowledge and expertise by teaching people remotely. This is typically done with Skype, text messages and other forms of communication to give people tailored advice about something you're knowledgeable about.

Consulting

Consulting is similar to coaching, but is more business-oriented. Consulting online operates just like consulting in person, except you're not limited by your physical location. You can give someone tax filing advice from halfway around the world, or teach them how to better use Facebook for their business, etc. - oftentimes at a premium price.

Software

This is something I have personal experience with selling and marketing. I did my internship at Languages Point in Turin, Italy and redesigned their homepage as well as English Learning ePlatform sales page (visible at www.languagespoint.it). It was a lot of work, but I created a landing page that highlighted the benefits of their English learning ePlatform and helped create four unique packages at different price points and different levels of access to the platform with the premium package allowing four Skype sessions with a teacher. All the products were completely digital - even the lessons could be done online. What kind of software or platform can *you* sell?

One thing you may notice about all of the above is that they're all mostly passive income strategies. In case you've never heard of passive income, it basically means making money while you sleep. You've put in the effort to create a product, carried out proper marketing strategies and have a platform to accept payments and deliver the product automatically. After that, all you need to do is sit back and relax! This is different than active income, contrastingly, where you trade your time for money. And, there are varying degrees of 'passivity'. For example, with this eBook, I may choose to simply upload it on Kindle Direct Publishing (KDP), gather a few reviews and call it good. Or, I may write a monthly blog post on high-authority websites and add a link to my eBook there to continue to gain traffic. You can be as hands off or *laissez-faire* as you wish.

As with the other strategies, you want to ensure your product is valuable. Whether you teach something from a unique perspective or create a customized plan for customers or have a great app you've developed, it needs to be worth your buyer's time and money. If not, you're going to earn a poor reputation, be left with negative feedback and deal with customer complaints. Don't go half-way in your efforts. Try not to hold back and share as much valuable information as you can. And again: you need a website or a third-party selling platform to sell your products.

Some of the best and most popular platforms people use to sell digital products include:

Udemy. Have something you want to share with the world? You can create an ecourse and sell it on Udemy.com. There are many other ecourse selling platforms available, but this tends to be one of the most popular options.

Skillshare. Skillshare is another great marketplace to sell digital courses. Unlike Udemy, which takes a certain percentage of your earnings depending on where buyers come from (i.e. directly from your marketing efforts or from their website), you earn money on Skillshare by gaining time spent on your eCourse and by selling premium memberships.

Flippa. Flippa allows users to buy and sell businesses - from blogs, to ecommerce shops and more. You can buy a website that's already set up online, or create one and sell it for others to buy - while making a profit, of course.

Teespring. You can sell anything anywhere with Teespring. Some of the most popular items include apparel, home decor, socks, phone cases, accessories and mugs. Basically, you create the design while Teespring supplies the production and shipping. It's easy!

Cafepress. Cafepress is very similar to Teespring. All you need to do is create the design, do a little marketing, and Cafepress worries about the rest. You can create clothing designs for men and women, houseware, accessories and more.

Amazon Kindle. Amazon's Kindle Direct Publishing makes it easy for you to create books from start to finish - all you need to do is provide the content. You can even sell physical printed books from their platform; they have an on-demand printing system.

Since these third-party websites take cuts in your profit, I highly recommend using your own website to sell your digital products in addition to these strategies since it's basically free. Just be sure to read the contract of each individual platform carefully. If you're planning on selling across multiple platforms, you want to obviously avoid exclusive contracts so that you're not limited to where you can sell. The disadvantage of creating a website or using your pre-existing one is that you're responsible for bringing in the traffic, meanwhile these third-party websites already have an established audience. And the audience isn't just there to browse; they're interested buyers. They know that these websites exist to sell - they're not just there to browse your free SEO blog post you created, for example, which is a major plus.

After making a sale, you don't want to keep your buyers hanging! Be sure to collect feedback from your valued customers and make changes to your course, website template, diet plan, etc. to improve it for others, if necessary. Creating digital products is always a game of trial and error. On top of receiving - and acting - upon feedback, you want to collect buyer reviews, just like physical products. Another strategy to implement is using a satisfaction guarantee. Chances are, if you've put in your blood, sweat and tears into creating your digital product, you won't have many returns (you should expect less than 1% if you've created value). But, there are always those customers that are hard to please. Instead of fighting with them, realize it's not worth the stress (nor is it worth jeopardizing your reviews and reputation). Instead, just give them their money back and let them go - you've got other customers who value what you've created, anyway! Hopefully difficult customers are the least of your concerns when implementing this Laptop Entrepreneur lifestyle. Selling digital products can be a great way to supplement your income - or even be your main source of income.

Quick Summary of Selling e-Products

1. Research, Research, Research. Are you noticing a pattern here? To save yourself from wasting time, you need to do your homework before writing an eBook on the best types of dog sweaters or the best restaurants in Antartica. You may personally be a huge fan of dog sweaters and own multiple for your pooch, but that doesn't mean others are. As for restaurants in Antartica - there's not much on the menu there, and therefore, not a significant amount of demand for that kind of eBook. Find something with demand that's profitable and figure out how to beat your competition.

2. Create a Digital Product Teaching or Selling Something You're Good At. Make use of your talents and create something that will benefit others. If you've studied a topic extensively, are naturally good at something, or are passionate about atopic - pursue it further. You can choose to write code, make a video, create a customized plan or just about anything else. The digital marketplace is waiting for your input! What can you add?

3. Focus on Providing Value. To avoid requests for returns and poor reviews, you want to ensure you've produced a quality product. That means checking for typos (sorry if there are any in this book! I tried my best to catch them, but I'm a one-man team. No fancy publishing company to back me!), working out the kinks in your platform, and ensuring you deliver what you advertise.

4. Create a Website and Market Your Product. You need to create a website that allows customers to make a purchase. But first, you'll need to do some convincing. This means creating a video explaining your product or writing enticing copy. Also, you need to focus on methods of bringing interested buyers to your website. And you can always explore the aforementioned digital marketplace platforms above to enhance your sales.

5. Follow Up With Your Customers. If you can, grab your customer's emails so that you can follow up with them. Collect their feedback on your product and see where you can improve. You'll also be able to market them for future digital products you create. And for buyers who were disappointed or are difficult to please, remember that sometimes it's best to bite the bullet and take a loss. It's not worth the time to argue with those rare sour customers.

Property Rentals

If you want to start a venture that's almost entirely hands-off and takes less marketing efforts and SEO tactics than the aforementioned methods, I recommend property rentals. But, as you can probably guess: you need property first (which can be a huge expense!). First of all, there are two approaches to making money via property rentals: you can go the **short-term** route (where you would rent your property for days to weeks to months) or the **long-term** route (renting your property for a year or longer). One thing you may find strange is that I listed this section under operating a virtual business even though it requires a physical space. But hear me out: even if you decide to go the short-term route, you can still find ways to automate the processes (e.g. check-in, cleaning, etc.) with a little creative effort and outsourcing. Many people - especially young people - are also hesitant to invest in property since they likely don't have much money saved up to begin with. Again: with a little creative planning, there are ways to get around that obstacle.

But, before you even start planning out your short or long-term rental in detail, you need to gain an overview. That means research, of course. What's the average **rental** price in a target area for a studio? What's the average price to **buy** a studio in that target area? Is there a significant demand for rentals? Or, is the market slower? Does the target area receive a large influx of tourists each year? How many and when? If you're unable to rent out your property for whatever reason in the future (e.g. changes in short term rental laws, lack of demand, etc.) would you still be able to bear the costs of the mortgage, property taxes and utilities? You need to ask yourself these types of questions and find concrete answers. Calculate the ratio between median rental prices and the price you would pay to buy a place each month. If by buying (rather than renting) you'd be saving hundreds or even thousands of dollars, perhaps you've found a nice rental market to get into.

After finding a profitable area and home structure to invest in (a studio apartment, three bedroom family house, etc.) it's time to figure out what kind of rental strategy you want to implement. Would you rather be more hands-on (even from a distance) to make more money? If so, renting on a short term website like **Airbnb** or **Homeaway** could be your best option. If you'd rather take a more hands-off (and potentially more secure) approach, you may consider renting with long-term contracts. Obviously, each option has its pros and cons.

With short term-rentals, you often churn through so many different people with so many different living habits that are hard to gauge - despite being able to see their reviews. That means your first 10 guests may be extremely pleasant and easy going, but that eleventh throws a party in your place or is loud and the police are called by neighbors, etc. Or, they may leave your place completely destroyed, taking extra hours to clean. There are ways to mitigate these risks, and Airbnb does have insurance for its users and ways to fine unruly guests, but it's still a bigger headache than dealing with just one person per year as you would with long-term rentals. But, of course with long-term rentals, you never know what could happen: after the one-year lease is up, you may find your carpet irreparably stained by cat pee and vomit, you may have accidentally rented to a drug user or someone cooking meth, etc. While certain laws exist to prevent these kinds of situations (for example, to rent one must show they have sufficient income) there's never a guarantee that the rental experience is always going to be smooth. It could end up costing you thousands in a battle in court.

On the flip side, you can make four times more with short-term rentals than you can with the traditional long-term rental strategy. And, that's after adjusting for expenses! But how can you manage your Airbnb listing and property while you're on the go? It's simple. You can decide to leave the cleaning duties to a friend, family member, college student or find a cleaning service to take care of it for you. Obviously, this will cost you money (and you need to ensure you find someone reputable and trustworthy!), but what do you gain? Your freedom, of course. Instead of cleaning out the apartment yourself, hiring someone else to do it for you can save you lots of time and prevent you from being tied down to one place. There's an even more convenient option for those who want to rent out their property entirely hands-off: you can enlist a property management service provider. Keep in mind that this eats into your profit margin significantly, with most property management agencies collecting 20 to 30% of all of your revenue. If you want to make a little more money, opt for hiring someone to clean your apartment independently. Now that you've got the cleaning situation figured out, what about the check-in process? There's a solution that's simple and effective: using a keypad door lock. That way, you can change the code on your door from wherever you are in the world, ensuring that your home is always safe. And, most people prefer this option anyway! It's always less of a hassle to do a self-check in than meet up with someone. This can help boost your rating, too. Think about it: if you're a visitor and your flight arrives two hours late and the AIrbnb owner isn't there to hand you the keys, you'd be pretty irritated (and so would the host!). That's why a self-check in method is best in ensuring your guests get inside whenever they arrive - and you or a delegated person don't have to be there physically to get them situated. Want to make the check-in process more personal? Consider making them a virtual check-in video with a quick tour of the house. Film a quick video showing them what they need to know about your property, what's going on nearby and how to get around.

After deciding on the rental strategy and finding the right people to make your short or long-term rental a success, you now need to market your property. I'm not going to go too much in depth for the long-term option since it's straight-forward. You can put an ad on Craigslist, Facebook or in the classified of your local newspaper. Depending on the demand, you should find someone fairly quickly (if you haven't priced the rent too high, of course). As for Airbnb or any other short-term rental platform, you want to make sure the images of your home are professional and well-lit (this is probably even more important than long-term rentals since you'll likely have so much competition. If you have to spend some money to get professional photos done, do it! It'll likely pay for itself). You also want to optimize your description and learn the basics of copywriting. Make sure the pictures capture their attention and the description seals the deal! You want your future guests to fall in love with the **idea** of staying at your place. One thing that many renters on AIrbnb often do is price their property lower for the first few stays. Why's that? You need to build up quality reviews. People are less-likely to pay full-price for a property that hasn't been vouched for. Also, be sure to collect feedback from your guests before they leave a review - that way you know what you can improve on for the future.

Once you've got some quality reviews lined up (at least five) it should be smooth sailing from there! You can focus on changing your pricing strategy and find what works best for you. But, just be sure to **expect the unexpected.** The power could go out at your property, you could get a few bad reviews from your listing which results in less buy activity, your cleaning person may not show up. Always be prepared for less than ideal situations. Hopefully nothing major happens to your property rental business while you're away, but just in case, it's important to have people you trust nearby should they ever need to visit the property or help in an emergency situation. On the bright side, this is unlikely to happen and property rentals are a consistent, stable way to make an income.

Quick Summary of Property Rentals

1. Research, Research, Research. Just because this business strategy is a bit different than the others doesn't mean you don't need to research! Find out about your local short-term rental laws, choose the right property type that will give you the best return, and find the best areas to invest in before you purchase blindly.

2. Decide On a Rental Strategy: Short Term or Long Term. After doing your homework, it's time to make a big decision: do you want to focus on making more profit, but having to deal with the rental business more actively? Choose the short-term strategy. Or, would you rather make a stable income from your property with less turnover? Then a long-term rental strategy is for you.

3. Make Sure Your Property is Clean, Maintained and Accessible. Whether you have a short term or long term property rental strategy, you will need to ensure the property is maintained. If the fridge stops working in both cases, you're likely the one liable to replace it. Make sure you have a trustworthy team of people and professionals who can help you out when things go wrong. Also, you need to focus on two important areas when utilizing the short-term rental strategy: cleaning and check-in. Figure out what works best for you - there are plenty of options to manage a short-term rental without having to be physically present.

4. Market Your Property. Marketing your property is another thing to think about. If opting for a long-term strategy, you'll likely have no problems listing the place yourself. If, however, you're doing a short-term strategy, you really need to put in extra care and attention in your listing. Remember: you're not just selling the four walls that make up your house; you're selling the idea of staying in your unique home. Use the product description to your advantage and be as clear as possible.

5. Always Be Prepared for Disasters. You never know when things are going to go south. Assemble a team of people you trust who can help you out when you're away. This also includes fining plumbers, electricians, and other service providers you can trust before you take off.

Don't Limit Yourself - Set Your Own Schedule and Be Free

The digital workforce is only going to increase in the future. More and more are realizing the benefits of working from home - or around the world. As I covered, from the worker's side, it's important to live life rather than live to work. That means working when you want to and taking time off to relax when you need to, too. From the employer's perspective, many are emphasizing soft skills and thus recognizing the importance of employee satisfaction. Allowing employees to work online means more productivity and job satisfaction. And, of course, the internet has allowed people to start their very own businesses that they can operate entirely from their laptop. Before working online becomes the norm, beat the crowds and reserve your space in the digital workforce as a Laptop Entrepreneur now!

ABOUT THE AUTHOR

I got started working online because I wanted to get a degree, debt-free. So I traveled to Italy to study Business Administration & Management and turned to the internet to make money for tuition. Outside of class, I spent my evenings working as a freelance writer (SEO copywriting, Amazon listing optimization & email marketing) and read a book each week to further my self-education and develop online marketing skills.

Since I've been able to pay for my tuition and bills from my freelancing online and travel the world, I wanted to share how others can do it, too. And so this book (and Journey On, which I wrote when I was 20 years old) was born!

Want to connect? Visit me at RyanScottSEO.com.

Sources

Alexander, et al. "The Digital Nomad Lifestyle: (Remote) Work/Leisure Balance, Privilege, and Constructed Community." *International Journal of the Sociology of Leisure*, Springer International Publishing, 1 Jan. 1970, link.springer.com/article/10.1007/s41978-018-00030-y.

Bullard, Alvern. "6 Most Profitable Blog Niches That Make The Most Money." *Success Unscrambled*, 10 Jan. 2020, www.successunscrambled.com/most-profitable-blog-niches/.

Butler, Josh. "Sydney Has The Second Most Unaffordable Housing In The World." *HuffPost Australia*, HuffPost Australia, 23 Jan. 2017, www.huffingtonpost.com.au/2017/01/23/sydney-has-the-second-most-unaffordable-housing-in-the-world_a_21661117/.

"Digital Nomads Ditch Cubicles for Shared Spaces, Choosing Their Co-Workers." *The Washington Post*, WP Company, 26 July 2009, www.washingtonpost.com/wp-dyn/content/article/2009/07/25/AR2009072500878.html.

Frost, Aja. "Dear Bosses Everywhere: The Case for 'Work From Home Fridays.'" *Job Search, Companies Hiring Near Me, and Career Opportunities*, The Muse, 30 Jan. 2015, www.themuse.com/advice/dear-bosses-everywhere-the-case-for-work-from-home-fridays.

"Have a Question?" *Upwork Help Center*, support.upwork.com/hc/en-us?flash_digest=69166ee63ef2b83a378e03425c6c2975dff11375.

Lee, Stephanie. "5 Unspoken Truths about Becoming Digital Nomads (Most Never Tell)." *GrowthLab*, 20 Sept. 2019, growthlab.com/what-i-wish-someone-told-me-before-becoming-a-digital-nomad/.

Liegl, Michael, and Desiree Bender. "Digital Nomading and the Care of Place." *Handbuch Soziale Praktiken Und Digitale Alltagswelten*, 2016, pp. 1–8., doi:10.1007/978-3-658-08460-8_24-1.

Michael, et al. "The 7 Ways to Escape the Rat Race." *Uncommon Dream*, 22 Feb. 2019, uncommondream.com/7-ways-to-escape-the-rat-race/.

Morgan, Blake. "NOwnership, No Problem: An Updated Look At Why Millennials Value Experiences Over Owning Things." *Forbes*, Forbes Magazine, 18 Jan. 2019, www.forbes.com/sites/blakemorgan/2019/01/02/nownership-no-problem-an-updated-look-at-why-millennials-value-experiences-over-owning-things/#403aa084522f.

Pinola, Melanie. "Can I Really Make a Living by Blogging?" *Lifehacker*, Lifehacker, 6 Mar. 2014, lifehacker.com/can-i-really-make-a-living-by-blogging-1537783554.

"Taxation in the United Kingdom/Corporation Tax/The Schedular System of Corporation Tax." *Taxation in the United Kingdom/Corporation Tax/The Schedular System of Corporation Tax - Wikibooks, Open Books for an Open World*, en.wikibooks.org/wiki/Taxation_in_the_United_Kingdom/Corporation_tax/The_schedular_system_of_corporation_tax.

"United States Federal Corporate Tax Rate." *United States Federal Corporate Tax Rate | 2019 | Data | Chart | Calendar*, tradingeconomics.com/united-states/corporate-tax-rate.

"Who's That Girl." *Esther Jacobs – the NO EXCUSES LADY: Speaker, Author, Digital Nomad*, 14 Feb. 2020, estherjacobs.info/en/whos-that-girl/.

"World Wide Web Technology Surveys." *W3Techs*, w3techs.com/.

www.ingramcontent.com/pod-product-compliance
Lightning Source LLC
Chambersburg PA
CBHW071419210526
45465CB00001B/456